Healing for the Inner Hurts

Dr. Jack Schaap

This book was the result of the combined efforts of two people: Dr. Bob Marshall and Mrs. Linda Stubblefield. Both have labored for many hours to make my thoughts and heart clear to the reader.

After earning his Bachelor of Science degree and Master of Pastoral Theology degree, Brother Marshall joined Dr. Schaap's staff at Hyles-Anderson College. He worked as Brother Schaap's assistant and taught Bible classes. When Brother Schaap accepted the pastorate of First Baptist Church, Dr. Marshall moved to the church where he now serves as an assistant pastor. He is married to Cyndilu Marshall, and they are the parents of five children.

Upon her graduation from Hyles-Anderson College in 1977, Linda Stubblefield began working for Marlene Evans with Christian Womanhood. After working in various capacities, she now serves as the assistant editor of the Christian Womanhood magazine. She is married to David Stubblefield, the academic dean at Hyles-Anderson College. The Stubblefields are the parents of two adult daughters.

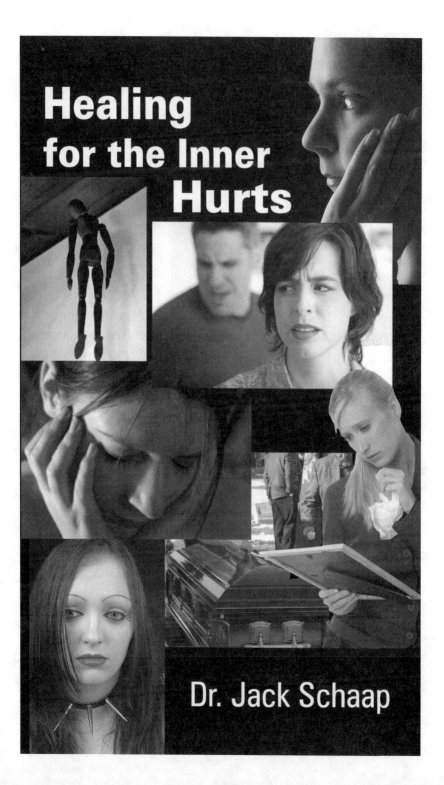

Healing
for the Inner
Hurts

Dr. Jack Schaap

CREDITS
Project Manager: Dr. Bob Marshall
Assistant: Rochelle Chalifoux
Transcription: Martha Gilbert
Page Design and Layout: Linda Stubblefield
Proofreading: Kelly Cervantes and Maria Sarver
Cover Design: Alex Midence

To order additional books by Dr. Jack Hyles,
please contact:
HYLES PUBLICATIONS
523 Sibley Street
Hammond, Indiana 46320
(219) 932-0711
www.hylespublications.com
e-mail: info@hylespublications.com

Dedication

Dedicated to the army of silent sufferers who masquerade as normal, functioning adults while nursing the inner wounds inflicted upon them from their days of youth.

You had your innocence stolen, your trust betrayed, and your love tainted by fear and pain. May you fully know the kindness and love of God our Saviour toward man.

May God grant you His grace and the will to break generational sins so that you may give to your posterity the hope of freedom and honesty in their spirit.

Table of Contents

Foreword

"Then said he unto the disciples, It is impossible but that offences will come: but woe unto him, through whom they come! It were better for him that a millstone were hanged about his neck, and he cast into the sea, than that he should offend one of these little ones. Take heed to yourselves: If thy brother trespass against thee, rebuke him; and if he repent, forgive him. And if he trespass against thee seven times in a day, and seven times in a day turn again to thee, saying, I repent; thou shalt forgive him." (Luke 17:1-5)

My purpose in writing this book is, of course, to help people, especially my very own church members, understand the complex issues facing them in life and to help provide a scriptural remedy for these issues. Job probably said it best in his declaration of the fate of man: *"Man that is born of a woman is of few days, and full of trouble. He cometh forth like a flower, and is cut down: he fleeth also as a shadow, and continueth not."* (Job 14:1, 2)

A man's days are full of trouble. Troubled pasts affect every relationship in life, and vicious cycles of abuse and neglect spawn even more abuse and neglect. Our lack of understanding of how to deal with these "offences" destines many to cycles of repetitive behavior unless this bondage is broken by healing the many inner hurts which life and the providence of God have dealt us.

My goal is to help my people with this book, but I understand that in a church the size I pastor, with tens of thousands of members, that they most surely represent a microcosm of the general public. These chapters will deal with delicate issues of life as well as with the heartaches and questions those heartaches generate. These situations need a pastor's wisdom and a Biblical remedy.

The year 2005 brought an incomprehensible event to the forefront in the daily newspapers and television newscasts. The unbelievable account seemed more than I could grasp! That, in America, we would allow those institutions which have a sacred trust to preserve life, to instead decide to terminate a life is inconceivable. According to their creed of professional behavior in the *Association of American Physicians and Surgeons, Inc.,* paragraph 3 of their code of conduct states: "The physician should not condone the taking of human life in the practice of his profession, *but at all times respect the sanctity of human life and seek to preserve or improve the quality of life.*"[1]

The motto *omnia pro aegroto* means "all for the patient." In his classical Hippocratic oath, which gave the medical profession a sense of duty to mankind which it never lost, Hippocrates vowed to do all to preserve life and never to assist in the destruction of life. Even recent graduates of American medical schools still swear an oath to preserve life. Hippocrates' principles of medical science were laid down 400 years before the birth of Christ, but they formed the foundation for the medical principles developed in the 1800s. Hippocrates required his students to take this oath. "The Oath of Hippocrates," holds the *American Medical Association's Code of Medical Ethics* (1996 edition), "has remained in Western civilization as an expression of ideal conduct for the physician."[2]

However, it would seem that we as Americans have reversed course and have callously allowed a woman to be starved to death. The general public sat back, watched, and allowed Terri Schiavo's indefensible death.

As I began developing the ideas for this book, I wanted to illustrate a Scriptural truth with that story as the backdrop. Allow me to make several introductory statements about the Terri Schiavo case. To be sure, I do not pretend to add to the material that has already been printed or spoken. Let me say on behalf of all of us who believe the King James Bible is the very Word of God: always choose life!

I am seeing a tendency that is barging—not creeping—into our fundamental circles, and that is the propensity we Christians somehow enjoy—the privilege of playing God. May I say that there are two ends to the spectrum of life. One end of the spectrum is a life that is a yet-to-be delivered baby; though some call it a "fetus" or a "tissue mass," that life is still a baby—a helpless, innocent infant incapable of caring for itself. The other end is a human being who becomes less and less responsive to the world around him. Both the young and the elderly do nothing much but sleep and eat. In truth, there's not a great difference between the two spectrums except for hope and anticipation. Of course, as believers, our hope does not end in death. Rather, death is the beginning of hope, not the ending of hope. Just like a delivery is the anticipation of a hope of life, death is also the anticipation of hope of life. As we watch life play out, we must be very careful not to play God on either end of the spectrum of life. There is a tendency among Christians to think that we have the right to decide matters of life and death. I have heard some very good Christians ably argue their cases.

In 2001 many Christians joined the Hyles' family in facing the passing of our former pastor and my father-in-law, Dr. Jack Hyles. When Brother Hyles' body was in the University of Chicago Hospitals, before he had been declared dead, I sat at his bedside. It was quite late, and members of the family were trying to rest in a nearby waiting room. As I sat in his room, I asked the attending nurse, "The machine that is bleeping his heartbeat is not really his heart beating, is it?"

"No," she said, "It's just a machine shocking his heart with an electrical pulse. Truthfully, in a few minutes, I need you to gather the family because a decision has to be made. We need to ask if you want to 'pull the plug.' " In that instance, it was not a matter of whether he was eating or breathing on his own. Brother Hyles was doing nothing on his own; he had already left this earth. To be sure, sitting at the bedside of Brother Hyles was a very different scenario than that of Terri Schiavo.

Very few of us have been faced with the difficult situation that Terri Schiavo's parents and her former husband had to face. Probably it would be best to leave to people who have walked those same paths the courtesy to address the difficulties and issues of having a family member whose life is very similar to Terri's— but very different from yours. I try to leave opinions in the hands of those who have the right to give them. Of course, my opinion would be to always choose life, but that does not allow me to sit in judgment of those who have had to make incredible, heart-rending decisions.

The second point I want to make about the Terry Schiavo matter is that family problems and long-past, unaddressed hurts ultimately forced a judge, who knew nothing about the people involved, to have to "play God." I believe America probably has some maverick federal judges and district judges who might need to be reminded that their power is limited. Thankfully, America does have a system of checks and balances in place.

When some judges blatantly make decisions which disregard laws, some investigation or consideration might well be warranted. However, before I sit in judgment over a particular judicial decision, I want to remind myself and others of what forced that judge to make that decision. Quite simply, a family could not function together and placed tremendous pressure on one another.

Many situations will arise in life where people who do not want to make certain decisions will be forced to do so because of dysfunctional family members. Two or more family members let hurts fester into a very infected, grievous wound. The greatest heartache came when a non-family member had to make the decision, an even greater hurt.

Thirdly, the problems in Terry Schiavo's life escalated because of an untreated, potentially fatal disorder. I want to be delicate, but those who read the articles and listened to the news understand that Terry Schiavo's problem resulted when her heart stopped, and the blood ceased flowing to her brain long enough to cause her debilitating condition. She suffered from an eating disorder with which many young ladies struggle. That disorder is, in many cases, the direct result of an inside hurt that has not been handled properly.

> As it is with self-inflicted violence, trauma is a common antecedent to eating disorders: Slightly more than one-third of individuals who have eating disorders also experienced some type of trauma, typically sexual abuse, as a child. Eating disorders, like SIV [self-inflicted violence], may stem from a need for an adequate coping mechanism or mechanism of gaining control.[3]

My goal is to prevent these kinds of scenarios from happening. Again, let me stress that the Terri Schiavo situation involved some unresolved painful and hurtful emotions that caused a rift in a family. Unfortunately, this fragmented family had to endure the press publishing their story in every nationwide avenue possible. To me, how the press treats struggling families in such an inopportune time seems very insensitive and very sacrilegious. Because this situation has been made into a national case, people do talk about it. Enormous emotional hurt was caused by the treatment of a helpless person. Terri Schiavo had become a helpless person, and however we, as a people, collectively decide to treat the Terri Schiavos of this world, is indicative of how we ultimately choose to sit in judgment of all helpless people. In the final analysis, we could well be, in some cases, determining our own fate when we have lost the capacity to make those choices for ourselves. Let us be very careful that we categorically always favor giving the helpless person a chance.

Whatever you decide—rightly or wrongly—in a particular situation is between you, your conscience, and God. On behalf of the helpless people—the nursing-home people and the educable slow, whose mental capacities range broadly from totally unable to comprehend what is going on around them to fairly bright and near normal, I am going to vote on the side of their being given a chance. All of these so-called "helpless" people are welcomed in First Baptist Church, and they add a welcome dimension to our church.

Time and again in our nursing home ministry, some people have come who talk to themselves and answer themselves as they converse with another person within themselves. They don't respond to the people around them, and they do not answer questions. Sometimes we may say, "Why do we even bring those people to this church?" Isn't it worth it when salvation brings deliverance from addictions, and some are now sitting in the services, clothed, and in their right mind? Addictions were holding these people captive and in bondage. Should we do less for these people than Jesus did?

In Mark 5, Jesus met a madman in the country of the Gadarenes who lived in a cemetery. If he was taken prisoner, he merely broke the chains that held him captive. *"...he was in the mountains, and in the tombs, crying, and **cutting** himself with stones."* Jesus freed him from the unclean spirits that held him captive. The townspeople came to see the man who *"...was possessed with* *the devil, and had the legion, sitting, and clothed, and in his right mind...."* Jesus made the difference!

If modern psychologists had been diagnosing people in Bible times, no doubt they would have labeled this man as having dissociative identity disorder (DID), formerly known as multiple personality disorder.

In many ways an individual with dissociative identity disorder is much like an extended family. Each of the 'family members' has a distinct personality with particular strengths and weaknesses. Dissociative identity disorder is generally related to intense trauma experienced as a child. Severe sexual or physical abuse as a child is a common antecedent of this disorder. Ritual abuse, which is often both intense and chronic, also has been related to dissociative identity disorder. Self-inflicted violence (SIV) serves many functions for people with DID. Just as violence sometimes exists in families, violence can occur between two identities contained in an individual. SIV is sometimes a violent act perpetrated by one alter on another. Many people with DID have at least one alter who is angry, violent, and abusive. These alters take their rage out on the other identities—and in reality, of course, their own physical selves.[4]

When Jesus came, the maniac of Gadara stopped abusing himself—cutting himself. He became a witness for the cause of Christ. *"...Go home to thy friends, and tell them how great things the Lord hath done for thee, and hath had compassion on thee."* The key word of this verse is compassion. Someone has to make a choice to give the hopeless and helpless ones a chance. If I have to make a mistake, I will be in the wrong on the side of giving these unwanted people a chance. Some will certainly disagree with me, but I would far rather err on the side of giving these people— God's people made in His image—a chance.

When members of First Baptist Church come to me seeking help with a terrible case of "marriage-itis," and they are about to "throw in the towel," I am going to believe in them. If I don't want to believe in them, I am going to believe that the God we serve is big enough to help them—just like He helped the maniac of Gadara.

If some parents come to me seeking help for a wayward teenager who has ruined their name and brought shame and reproach on their family, I am still going to believe in him. If I cannot believe in him, I am going to believe in them. If I cannot believe in them, I am going to believe in a God Who is big enough to transform their family.

I am going to give the people who cross my path a chance! The more hopeless the person is, the more he needs someone who is strong enough to say, "I am in your corner! I am on your team."

CHAPTER ONE

Healing for the Inner Hurts

Prerequisite Reading
Philippians 4:1-13

An alarming crisis has been unfolding in the youth of the world for several years. Quite possibly this exigency could be considered pandemic, or at least epidemic, since this issue is being observed on a worldwide scale. This disorder affects 2.5 to 3 million[1] youth in America alone. In the United Kingdom, entire ministries are established to cope with its effects upon their youth. Samaritan Ministry indicates that 43% of the UK's population knows someone who is affected by a condition known as "self-hurting."[2] Although self-hurting occurs primarily in youth ages 13 to 18, it has received notoriety because of the esoteric lives of young adults like Princess Diana. Often called "self-harm" or "cutters," the condition is also known as "Deliberate Self-Harm Syndrome," and is described as follows:

> The National Mental Health Organization states that self-injury is also termed self-mutilation, self-harm or self-abuse. The behavior is defined as the deliberate, repetitive, impulsive, non-lethal harming of one's self. Self-injury includes: cutting, scratching, picking scabs or interfering with wound

healing, burning, punching self or objects, infecting oneself, inserting objects in body openings, bruising or breaking bones, and some forms of hair-pulling, as well as other various forms of bodily harm.[3]

Self-mutilation is defined by Dr. Armanda Favazza, a professor of psychiatry at the University of Missouri at Columbia Medical School and author of *Bodies Under Siege*, the first book to explore self-mutilation, as "the direct, deliberate destruction or alteration of one's own body tissue without conscious suicidal intent.[4]

In the last four years, many young ladies from the age of 11 through college age have come to my office for counsel because of SIV (self-inflicted violence). Many have fresh wounds and scars covering their forearms. In some cases, a lady counselor or the young lady herself will admit that she has similar and fresh wounds elsewhere. These young people have developed a terrible habit of doing what they call "cutting themselves." I would not be at all surprised if a hundred or more teenagers who attend our public services at First Baptist Church engage in cutting themselves.

The February 2006 issue of *Reader's Digest* focused on this disorder in an article entitled "Thrills That Kill."

Though not as common as anorexia—approximately 7 million females and 1 million males suffer from eating disorders—cutting is a growing epidemic among teenage girls. Experts who study self-injury estimate that as many as one out of every 200 teen girls hurt themselves, resulting in 2 million reported cases per year. "Because of the awareness created by these websites [cutting websites that promote self-injury]," says CPYU.org's Mueller, "cutting has gone from being a way to cope to the hip thing to do." In fact studies suggest that there are 3 million self-injurers in the United States. Two million of them cut or burn themselves, while the other million hit, brand, scar, or excessively pierce themselves. "People who cut themselves believe they are horribly flawed in some way," says Wendy Lader, clinical director of S.A.F.E. Alternatives, a referral and treatment program for self-injurers. "It makes them feel strong. They think, 'I'm not like the rest of you. I'm tough. I can tolerate pain or starvation better than you.' But no matter how much they cut or starve themselves, they're not dealing with the real issue—their out-of-control emotions."[5]

For this meticulous ritual of cutting, some teens have a quite a collection of knives, pins, and razor blades. They store their cutting instruments in a very special, usually hidden, place. They write letters or pour out their heart to me in an appointment. I listen to them as they tell me about their ritual of making numerous cuts and hurting themselves intentionally and deliberately until they bleed. So often when their behavior is discovered, they are brought to me with the statement, "Pastor, I have no idea how to help this person."

The majority of people who hurt themselves were hurt by others when they were children, suffering physical, sexual, or emotional abuse. A nineteen-year-old college sophomore relates, "I hurt myself so that I can feel the pain of now, of today. I'd rather feel pain from now, that I'm creating, than the pain from my past...I was abused pretty bad as a kid." SIV can be a way to replicate the original abuse, to establish control, to provide self-punishment, to express emotional pain, or some combination of several or all of these things. If you engage in self-inflicted violence, chances are pretty good that you were abused as a child.[6]

In about four or five sentences, I can identify quite carefully and closely with these hurting young people just by talking and explaining why they are cutting themselves.

"Academic studies commonly report self-injurers feel empty inside, over- or under-stimulated, unable to express their feelings, lonely, not understood by others, and fearful of intimate relationships and adult responsibilities. Self-injury is their way to cope with or relieve painful or hard-to-express feelings and is generally not a suicide attempt. But relief is temporary, and a self-destructive cycle often develops without proper treatment."[7]

Many people will never seek help because their habit is embarrassing. They would never want to talk with their pastor or a counselor. Because they do not tell anyone, they live in a private world of self-inflicted pain from which they would love to be delivered. However, they cannot find deliverance.

The Cycle of Self-Inflicted Violence

Self-inflicted violence is not a one-time event. It often becomes a way of coping with life. Unpleasant feelings, such as anger and fear of abandonment, lead to a state of emotional tension. This tensions requires the use of coping techniques. Some people develop the unhealthy coping technique of self-mutilation, which relieves the built-up tension. Relief becomes a positive reinforcer for the self-mutilation.[8]

The person who self-mutilates may feel better for the moment, but feelings of shame and self-reproach may soon follow the immediate sensation of relief. The shame leads to more emotional tension, and the cycle repeats.

Self-mutilation is a way to express feelings such as shame,

rage, and fear. It is also a way to cover up feelings by substituting physical pain for emotional pain. The teenager wants both to discharge unbearable feelings and to bury them. Self-mutilation is a way to gain control over their feelings. Self-mutilators make themselves feel what they want to feel. Other people may have the power to make them feel hurt or ashamed, but they have the power to inflict pain. They simply inflict it on themselves. A person who self mutilates may think it is not acceptable to rant and rave when angry. He chooses to quietly express his anger by cutting himself. He does it in secret because expressing anger is not allowed in the household. He has gained a sense of control.[9]

Sometimes college-age or young ladies in their early twenties come to my office or to another counselor in our ministry, and the problem they share is very similar to what Terri Schiavo had—a potentially life-threatening eating disorder. An eating disorder like anorexia nervosa or bulimia is nothing to laugh at, to tease about, or mock. Girls struggle with these eating disorders for very real reasons, and these diseases are a form of self-inflicted violence.

Anorexia nervosa is characterized by behavior directed losing weight, peculiar patterns of handling food, an intense fear of gaining weight, disturbance of body image, and is unremitting until death.[10]

The causes for self-hurting varies, but commonalities exist among this group of people who experience such tremendous inner hurting, and they struggle to find an avenue of expression. Many of these self-hurters have an enormous load of baggage they have carried for years, such as a major change during their adolescent years; parental marriage difficulties; divorce; the loss of a parent to death; physical, sexual, or emotional abuse; family violence; emotional distresses of fear, hurt, or anger; rejection or welfare insecurities; or no personal control in their life. These hurting young people long to express outwardly what they have been struggling with inwardly. Their only avenue of escape to cope with their feelings is to express anger toward themselves. Their only way to feel alive and real is to feel pain on the outside instead of the inside. More than likely during episodes of abuse, the person felt violated, helpless, and powerless, with little or no control over his environment or his body. SIV may be a way of recreating some of the violence a person...

> endured or witnessed as a child, allowing him to reenact the trauma through self-injury. Replicating previous traumatic experiences allows the person to symbolically alter the original course of the abuse because, when the individual performs these self-injurious acts, he has control. By using SIV, he is able to go from a situation in which he felt helpless and powerless to a situation in which he has complete control, autonomy, and power.[11]

I do not have a simple answer for this problem which is secretly permeating our society. For numerous people in our midst, life is far more complicated than we can imagine. Many of us were fortunate enough to have been taught, or else we have learned, how to deal with the injustices or the unexpected regrettable events of life.

Teenage girls and young women are not alone in experiencing the inner hurts that affect the stability of life. "Both men and women intentionally injure themselves. In fact, the proportion of men and women who engage in SIV is roughly equal."[12] An equal number of young men come to my office seeking understanding and an avenue to express their deep inner confusion and hurt. In particular, I am thinking of an 18-year-old boy who is not, nor ever has been, a member of First Baptist Church of Hammond.

However, he is typical of some other young men who have sought counseling. This particular young man said, "I have reached a point where I have to talk to someone, and I chose the one person I felt would not laugh at me. I felt you would at least give me a hearing before you said, 'I'm sorry. I can't help you.'"

As I listened to his story unfold, I marveled at how this young man had managed to come this far.

He continued, "When I was about 11 or 12, just beginning junior high, my parents decided they wanted to toughen me up a little bit. They decided sending me to a boy's military academy would be good. I hated the thought of it, but I didn't have any input, so I was shipped to an all-boys' military academy. As soon as school was out on my first day, a group of high school boys grabbed me, took me to a fence line on the edge of the property where there were no cameras and no people to see us, and they gang-raped me. The whole incident was so shocking to my senses I could not deal with it.

"That went on every day for six years. They threatened to kill me if I ever told. They took a little rabbit in their hands, pulled off its head, and warned me, 'We'll do that to you if you tell.' That threat makes a powerful impression on you. When you are 12 years old, and big boys hurt you that badly, it deeply affects how you think.

"I came to you today not because I'm necessarily angry at those boys any longer, but because I have become what I hated in them. I am a bona-fide sodomite. Committing sodomy is as natural for me as breathing air. I have had multiple relationships with scores of men and boys. Mine has become a lifestyle, and I hate myself so much I cannot deal with me any more. I hate my father for sending me to a place where that could happen to a boy. I hated those boys, but now I am one of them. To hate them is to hate me. I don't really think you have any answers for me, but I would love to know—why do these kinds of things happen? Why do I have to live in this prison of hell? Why do I have to be a sodomite?

"To sit in a typical church service is just opening myself to get reamed out, just to get terribly crucified, to be castigated as an outcast, and to be pushed out! I know how the Bible describes my kind. But I am some man's son. I should be some woman's husband. I should be attending your college and studying the Bible, but I know I am not welcome there, and I know why. Obviously you cannot allow a person like me in the boys' dorm because that's like putting a feast in front of a starving man. If you put me in the girls' dorm, they would be safe; but I know you cannot do that either.

"I don't fit in anywhere! So, before you worry about your politically correct answer to me, when I leave you after this meeting, I will never come back to see you. I did not come for help for me. I came on behalf of the teenage boys who are being abused today somewhere and to tell you that you should do something about it.

"I have now hurt little boys who were the same age as I was when those boys hurt me. I think nothing of it. I don't even think about the boy because I am hurting me. I want to hurt someone, and the only way to do that is to hurt another boy."

> The most important thing in communication is to hear what isn't being said.
> –Peter F. Drucker

We chatted for a little while longer, and after our appointment was over, I wrote down a statement: **Those who hurt us the most are often hurting the most.** If you work in my kind of business, you will meet and work with every imaginable hurt in the world—from murder, pedophilia, lesbianism, to sodomy. You will counsel people guilty of every stripe of sin—living with every imaginable kind of addiction. You will discover one profound fact: the people who are doing all the hurting are some of the people who are hurting the most. May I remind you that the painful truth is that every time I address a certain category of sin, anywhere from a dozen to a hundred names and/or faces go through my mind of people who I am trying desperately to restore and to redeem.

It is so easy for those of us who are very opinionated to have strong opinions about Terri Schiavo and her former husband. After all, he is still alive and now married to the woman with whom he was living. He has two children with his former mistress. We look at the $1.5 million life-insurance settlement he received and form some strong opinions. If that man called me on the phone today and said, "Pastor Schaap, I have no place in the world to go to where people don't think the worst of me," I would say, "Come to Hammond, come to my office, and I will help you." Everyone needs someone who will give them a chance. Everyone needs some place where he can go and be accepted.

We Christians still must take a position that, to some degree, everyone is responsible for putting Christ on the cross. Our sins put Jesus on that cross just as surely as the judge, Terry Schiavo's former husband, Terri Schiavo, her parents, the attorneys, and Congress did. Nobody will ever stand before Jesus Christ and say, "I am the exception. They are the ones whose sins put You on the cross—not me." No! Like the Negro spiritual says, "It's me, it's me, it's me, O Lord, standing in the need of prayer." Be gentle and kind with people—no matter how much you disagree with them and no matter where you stand. Brother Hyles always said, "There is never a time to be unkind."

Labeling others often builds walls that should not be built. Be careful about labeling other Christians with a denominational tag. To be sure, I remind the people who regularly attend First Baptist Church of Hammond that we are Baptists. I am a Baptist preacher, and I believe in hellfire and damnation preaching. However, there must be a place of refuge that says to a hurting one, "We are as narrow-minded as the cover on the King James Bible from which I preach, but between the covers of that Book there is room for every human being—including you and me." If room cannot be found for everyone, then I want to get a different religion. If the God we serve is a God Who excludes certain people because of tags or labels or sins, then we do not have the right God! Every human being needs a God Who says, *"Whosoever will, let him take the water of life freely."* (Revelation 22:17) Thank God we serve a God Who *"...so loved the world, that He gave his only begotten Son, that whosoever believeth in him should not perish, but have everlasting life."* First Baptist Church of Hammond, Indiana, is in the business of working with the people who don't fit in any other place.

I grieve for those people who place their confidence and security in a man. In 2005 Pope John Paul II died after a lengthy, debilitating illness. Tens of thousands traveled to the Vatican City to pay their respects and to look for new leadership. I grieve for those good people because they need to know the truth, and they desperately need the security that Jesus offers.

We cannot write off these misdirected people. By all means, we must take a stand and know what we believe, but we cannot afford to write off people. Those who often hurt us the most—an abusive father who has anger management problems—does not need a son to write him off. Perhaps that father even goes to church and wears a mask of godliness. As a son, you know he is abusive. May I remind you that just because he goes to church does not necessarily mean that he has dealt with the inward anger hurting him. I have observed this recurring pattern for years. Every man with whom I have counseled who either abuses his wife or his children is a man who has indelible hurts from his childhood. He has never dealt with those issues.

I realize that when a boy becomes a man, he is supposed to deal with those anger issues. Unfortunately, for various reasons, some are never able to deal with the past. Let me be the Devil's advocate, if you will, at this juncture. I have yet to find a pedophile whose life was not interrupted by a severe injury on his boyhood journey to manhood. The injury never healed in his youth, and as a result, his unhealed hurt hurts other adolescent and teenage boys. "In an inpatient sample of convicted rapists and child molesters, 92% had experienced past trauma. The most common form of trauma experienced was child sexual abuse."[13]

Another source stated,

> As many as one in three women has experienced significant sexual or physical abuse by age twenty-one. Sexual and other forms of abuse early in life can damage self-esteem and create negative self-images.[14]

However, these and other extenuating circumstances **never** make victimizing another human being acceptable. Being victimized will **never** be a satisfactory reason for victimizing others.

It is incredibly easy for mankind to stand on our little soap box and judgmatically point a finger at a pedophile. I understand that in prison other hardened prisoners will try to maim or kill a pedophile. For this reason, most convicted pedophiles are kept separate from other prisoners. These prisoners—who are guilty of every kind of criminal behavior, even murder—say, "We don't like 'your kind.' " However, "that kind" is "that kind" because nobody stepped in and helped him when he was unable to defend himself. From his youth he bears the emotional as well as the physical scars, and they boil inside him without an avenue of release, a friend to help him, or an ear to hear.

Those who sit in judgment righteously say, "Well, he's a big boy now. He should get over it."

May I ask, "Why don't **you** get over **your** problems?" Many a person does not have any problem with justifying his outbursts of temper which cripple the emotions of those who have to hear the tirade. Many others have no problem justifying their smoking addiction, or liquor addiction, or drug addiction, or living with a member of the opposite gender. It's amazing how easily some can justify their own damnable, abominable, heretical sins while pointing a crooked finger at someone else and saying, "We don't want **your kind** here."

Certainly, I do not want a convicted pedophile working at our kids' camps! At First Baptist Church we ask every volunteer to submit to a background check because I want to protect our ministry. We do our homework before allowing anyone to assume a position of working with people, especially children, in our ministries. As the pastor, I am accountable to Jesus Christ and to every parent who allows their children to attend our church.

We have no "black lists" in First Baptist Church of Hammond. This is a ministry of healing, and the person who is in trouble has an altar available to him where a Saviour is waiting with open arms. The God we serve specializes in forgiveness, grace, and mercy.

We have had people whom I dearly love in our ministry who have been forbidden to step foot on school property or be in any children's ministry. I counsel and meet with these people. I explain to them very kindly that we simply cannot take the risk. We read Scripture together; we pray together; we work together; and I search for ways to help everyone who wants help. I never want to look at someone designed by the hand of God and say, "I'm sorry! We can't help you." If First Baptist Church of Hammond, or any church for that matter, ever stops helping people, then I believe we have forfeited our charter as a church and as servants of Christ.

A certain couple whose marriage was failing miserably came for counseling. The husband was abusive in his treatment of his wife. The wife was ready to call a lawyer and start divorce proceedings.

After I listened to the criticisms, I asked the husband, "What happened to you when you were an adolescent boy that makes you so hateful? Who introduced you to pornography? Who showed you pictures that your young mind couldn't quite comprehend? Who showed you images and shared filth with you? I have no doubt the incident or series of incidents shocked your pre-developed fences so much that you don't know how to deal with women. As a result of this abuse, to you, women are to be used. When you are finished using them, you take the 'magazine,' throw it away, and say, 'I hate this!' Then you return to it, and the vicious cycle repeats. You lust, indulge, despise, and discard."

This man is now an adult, but when it comes to caring for his wife, he is still a confused, frightened boy. As a result, he mistreats his wife, perhaps his own daughters, and women in general.

It is unnatural for this man to hold such angry feelings toward the opposite gender. Not only is it unnatural, it is ungodly and unscriptural for a person to have such an intense distrust for the opposite gender. A loved one shattered his family with despicable behavior, and his actions wounded this adolescent so badly he still bears the scars today. Because he has not learned to deal with the shame and hurt, his spouse is bewildered by his angry, belligerent, unfounded behavior.

Allow me to make several practical statements to help protect the minds of your young people:

1. Keep young children and teens innocent and naïve. I am not afraid of our children learning about life in the proper timing and in a scriptural method. I fear that too many young people receive their sex education in the back of a school bus or on a senior trip. These forays into the facts of life once began in the sixth or seventh grade. Today, fourth and fifth-grade kids seem to know so much about intimacies that they have absolutely no business knowing! I contend there is a right way to explain those issues as well as a right timing for sharing them.

I personally love the illustration written by Corrie Ten Boom, the author of *The Hiding Place*. Miss Ten Boom was a member of a Dutch family who lived in the Netherlands during World

War II. Her family committed an unpardonable offense against the occupying Germans: they kept and hid Jews in a hiding place in their home. Eventually, the Gestapo caught them, and the Ten Booms were sentenced to concentration camps. However, Corrie's miraculous story of survival is not the story I wish to share.

Before the years of imprisonment, when she was a little girl and on through her teenage years, Corrie and her father took a trip every other month. Her father was a clock maker by trade, and he would travel to distant cities by train on business. For these trips, he would alternate taking Corrie and her sister. The two would spend several days working at that distant place and then return home.

When Corrie ten Boom reached her mid-teenage years, she told her father that she was no longer a child. "Father," she said, "I want to know about the facts of life."

A thoughtful man, Mr. Ten Boom was quiet and didn't answer her. Corrie became very bold about the matter. "Father, I don't mean to make you uncomfortable," she pressed, "but I want to know about the facts of life."

Her father finally replied, "Corrie, when we take our trip to the city every other month, who carries your luggage?"

Mystified by his reply, Corrie answered, "You do, Father. Please don't avoid the issue. All my friends but me know, and I feel so left out. I really wish to know about the facts of life."

"Corrie, when you take that trip with me every other month, who carries your luggage?"

"Father, I already answered that question," an exasperated Corrie replied, "You do!"

Her father nodded his head and said, "That's right, Corrie."

A few minutes later, Corrie posed her question again. "Father, will you please tell me about the facts of life?"

"Corrie, when we take that trip,…" Mr. Ten Boom began.

"Father," Corrie interrupted, "I know! You carry the luggage!"

"But why do I carry the luggage, Corrie?"

"Because it's too heavy for me to carry myself," she started at her reply. Realization flooded her mind.

"That's good, Corrie," her father agreed. "The time will come for you to know all the wonderful things about life, but right now, please let your Papa carry the luggage. I'll carry it until you have to carry it by yourself."

Sad to say, we have a generation of children and young people growing up who are much too knowledgeable. They watch television programs featuring 12-year-old mega-stars who earn salaries of $500,000 or more a week flaunting their bodies, eagerly sharing their stories of conquest, and discussing with whom they are having intimate relationships. Do you really want these immoral icons to be sex education teachers for your child?

We live in a crazy world which has captured and marketed sexuality, and as a result, has perverted a beautiful relationship. Sexuality is supposed to be a symbolic relationship of how much God loves us. The intimate marital relationship is also a symbolic statement that teaches how a man gets saved. *"Neither is there salvation in any other: for there is none other name under heaven given among men, whereby we must be saved."* (Acts 4:12) Jesus said, *"...I am the way, the truth, and the life: no man cometh unto the Father, but by me."* (John 14:6)

One Saviour with one way of salvation is symbolically revealed through an intimate act called the marriage union. Because the world does not understand that truth, that truth is abused, perverted, and distorted. That perversion of the truth is the reason why we have pedophiles, adulterers, and fornicators, to name a few. I beg you: keep your children naïve! Keep your kids simple-minded on these matters; they don't have to know everything. Children need to allow their parents and their pastor to carry the luggage.

Don't withhold the facts when the proper time comes. My wife and I chatted with our daughter after she and Todd were engaged. The naivete of our daughter was so refreshing.

Teach them how to be masters of the craft of marriage at the proper time. Keep in mind that driving privileges come at age 16. Voting privileges come at age 18. Driving a car and voting are minuscule matters of life compared to the sacredness of marriage. Parents need to carry the heavy baggage of the sacredness of marriage until their young people are mature enough to handle it. By the way, parents should know more about the sanctity of marriage than any school buddy knows.

One of the main reasons to keep children and young people ignorant and naïve is because they get hurt by their premature knowledge and cannot cope with the hurt. Adolescent girls and boys do not know how to properly carry this kind of information in life. I don't care what SIECUS (an organization designed to promote the sex education program of the public schools) or the National Endowment for the Arts or the National Education Association or any other purveyor of untruth alleges! Eleven- and twelve-year-old boys and girls do not have the spiritual strength or the emotional strength needed to handle the sexual dialogue of today's radio and television programming. We must declare war against this issue, or we will lose a generation of young people.

2. Don't ignore the classic danger signs of abuse in a child. Negative behaviors that signal a pressing problem include, but are not limited to, a sudden dramatic withdrawal from parents, a private fantasy world of anger, and punishing other little children or pets or inanimate objects (like dolls). I am not referring to a good, honest fistfight between brothers over a toy. I am addressing a violent display of hostility toward pets or little children. Evidence of fear and pairing off with a much older person of the same gender are also danger signs. Be open to the obvious signs of abuse.

As a pastor, I have taken the liberty of calling some parents to my office to say frankly, "Just some pastoral advice: watch your children. I have noticed they are pairing up with certain people with whom I would never trust my children."

If the parents say, "Oh, that's no problem," reiterate that **it is** a problem! That type of friendship is **not** natural. Friends should be friends with the same type of person they are or are becoming.

When I was working with my dad, I enjoyed the camaraderie of his friends—but **only** when my dad was around. Many of his employees were my relatives. Even though my parents trusted them, I was almost never alone with any of them; usually my mom or my dad were in the immediate area. I always gravitated toward my father's generation. I had a mind that wanted to hear ideas, solve problems, and think constructive thoughts as opposed to making stupid talk. That was just the way my personality was. Dad and Mom NEVER let me go with any older man with whom they wouldn't have trusted their very life's soul. Even then, it was a very rare occasion. Parents should always be aware of the danger signs of child abuse.

3. **Don't allow your hurt to become an excuse for your failures.** We are a hurting generation, but it is time for our generation to start searching for answers and stop looking for excuses! Yes, since the emergence of the "do-your-own-thing" 60s generation, our children are scarred from abuse, rape, liquor, recreational drug use, addictions, adultery, fornication, etc. Our present society is very aware of the degradations heaped on our children; we just don't know that the Devil is the author of all this misery and wretchedness. The world is wide open with its display of knowledge, and that knowledge wreaks havoc in the lives of many. Because so many are the products of this abusive society, they look for answers in all the wrong places. The excuses for the continual failure to put aside self-destructive behavior are rampant!

It is time to stop looking for an excuse because the Devil will provide one! Sin and Satan provide any number of excuses. The world is filled with too many excuses.

One of the great hurts that many people hold tightly within the confines of their heart is an injustice suffered. Someone hurts them, and unfortunately, the perpetrator is never caught. An even greater injustice occurs when a 14-year-old girl goes to her mother and says, "Dad (or uncle or brother or stepbrother or stepfather or ___) is doing things to me that he shouldn't be doing to me." Instead of believing her daughter, the mother covers for her husband and says, "Don't tell anyone!" or "You must have provoked him!" That mother failed her daughter as surely as her father violated her! An offense of that magnitude cannot be swept under a rug. That experience will come back to haunt that 14-year-old girl until she is 34 years old, losing her marriage, and doesn't understand why. The injustice of that terrible situation is that the perpetrator went unpunished; the daughter was punished!

Everyone knows in his heart that if a hurtful, emotional wrong is forced on an innocent human being, the perpetrator of that crime needs to pay for his evil doing. When the guilty go unpunished, the innocent suffer. That is one reason why young girls get a knife, open the blade, retreat to the privacy of a room where the light is very dim, and cut themselves until the blood flows. "They cut themselves to feel physical pain that will overshadow their emotional pain."[15] Every time a teen cuts herself, she is trying to punish the person who never got punished; along the way, she has begun to take the blame for the wrong. "I must have been very wicked or that person would not have done that to me," becomes a prevalent thought.

One of the things that children lay claim to is their own body, believing that their body is their own, and no one else is allowed to use, touch, or disturb it without permission. However, sexual or physical abuse leads to confusion over these very basic rules of ownership. Children who have been abused learn that their body is able to be hurt or manipulated by others. They learn that their bodies are not their own—that their boundaries are variable or nonexistent. Self-inflicted violence allows people to experience their body as their own.[16]

I have yet to meet anyone who cuts himself who does not believe he is the one who is primarily responsible for the hurt inflicted on him. Why? **Because a sense of justice is postponed, and justice postponed becomes perverted justice.** A person doesn't just stop thinking that a perpetrator should be punished.

It has been reported that more than half of all individuals who engage in SIV were abused—physically, sexually, and/or emotionally—as children. Often people who have been abused, incorrectly blame themselves for the abuse or believe they 'deserve' it because of their behaviors, thoughts, or feelings. People who engage in SIV are often overly critical of themselves.[17]

As a result, the person starts punishing himself and sometimes escalates to others: a spouse or children. Truthfully, it is not particularly helpful for a person to physically harm himself as a method of punishment. The person who punishes himself does not change his past, nor will it change the present. A person who hurts himself may feel better at the moment, but SIV cannot change the past; and many of the thoughts, feelings, or behaviors for which a person punishes himself may not, in fact, be culpable. As a person hurts himself and others, he is, in a twisted sense, trying to punish the unpunished violator.

A dad abused his child and seemingly got by with it. An older brother raped his teenage sister and got away with it. An unassuming little boy was abused by an older man, and the man went unpunished. A hurt and a wound occurred, and justice dictates

Self-injury can be an expression of anger or rage. For individuals who feel very helpless in their lives and feel unable to have any control over what happens to them, self-injury can be an expression of personal power as if to say, "It's my body and this is one thing I do have a say about." One dilemma with this expression of personal power is that it too often repeats, in some form, something that was done to that person during a trauma.[18]

that someone must be punished. When the perpetrator went unpunished, the violated one will eventually punish himself or another because punishment is a necessary part of justice.

This violation explains the conflict, the inner strife, and the often unexplainable mood swings and outbursts. A wrestling match is taking place inside a violated person trying desperately to find a stable platform of justice that cannot be found. Justice is like a seesaw. These hurting ones lash out at others with no provocation, and it becomes very difficult to reconcile "I thought you loved me," with the undeserved, unexplained abuse.

People who have these unexplainable, emotional outbursts are dealing with the inner hurts that have never been resolved. Someone got by with hurting another and successfully evaded punishment. For this reason, it is so important that parents pray for their children to get caught and receive punishment for even the smallest of violations, so they learn to have a sense of justice.

The only cure for injustice is forgiveness. When the person who committed the violation didn't get caught and punished, the only Scriptural way to handle the issue is forgiveness. Luke 17:4 says, "*And if he trespass against thee seven times in a day, and seven times in a day turn again to thee, saying, I repent; thou shalt forgive him.*"

Take special note of what Jesus said just two verses earlier: "*It were better for him that a millstone were hanged about his neck, and*

he cast into the sea, than that he should offend one of these little ones."
The purport of this verse is that the offender "gets by with it."
Jesus was saying, "When a little one gets hurt or injured by another, it would be better for that wrongdoer to have a millstone hung around his neck and be dropped in the water to drown." Everyone would no doubt say, "He got what he deserved." Obviously the general public cannot hang millstones around a person's neck or attach cinder blocks to his feet and throw him off a bridge, or the law will probably charge them with vigilantism or attempted murder. So what do you do when the guilty one should have a millstone hung around his neck and drowned? What do you do when you can't do anything about a terrible miscarriage of justice?

> The deepest wounds a person bears not to the body, but to the soul. The physical wounds a person bears will heal in short order, but wounds to the soul may take a lifetime.
> –Attila the Hun
> *Leadership Lessons*

Jesus, one of the greatest teachers of forgiveness, said, "You forgive them." Jesus lived in an eye-for-an-eye, tooth-for-a-tooth world. The word Jesus used for forgiveness was to "let go" or "untie." When a person forgives, he has let go of his imaginary, albeit painful control of the way he thinks things should be. Forgiveness means to untie ourselves from the burden of judging the way the situation is. "Forgiveness is a direct route to freedom, lightening up, and moving on."[19] When you do not see justice prevail and you do not have the authority or power to punish, the only power you have is to forgive.

When the disciples responded to Jesus' admonition, *"And the apostles said unto the Lord, Increase our faith,"* they were basically saying that they were having a very difficult time believing the principle He was teaching! Jesus' instruction to forgive was a revolutionary concept in that period of history.

Forgiving the person who wreaked havoc in your life can be

very demanding; Jesus did not say it would be easy. The truth is that the struggles you face may have very limited options; offering forgiveness may well be your only option. The word *forgiveness* scripturally means "to let go." Forgiving means, "I give for another's sake."

Scripturally, forgiveness is saying, "I release you, not for my sake—not for the sake of the person you hurt. I release you for His sake." Forgiveness is an act of the will where the victim says, "My God is bigger than your hurt, bigger than my hurt, and I forgive you for His sake; I let go of my hurts for His sake."

Hanging onto hurt will infect you, corrupt you, and ultimately destroy you. Holding fast to past hurts will defile everything around you: your marriage, your family, the people you love, and your friendships. Forgiveness requires a lot of faith and a very big God.

To be sure, forgiveness is not just a simple, one-time human action. Forgiveness is as much of a process as any part of the

Christian life. A doctor named Viktor Frankl, who was caught in the horrors of the Holocaust, learned the importance of being free from the corruption of hurt.

Viktor Frankl, M.D., had everything and everyone in his life taken from him, historically, the most appalling way possible. He is a survivor of the Holocaust. While in the concentration camp, Dr. Frankl realized one essential truth: no matter what they put him through, he still had within him the power to choose how he was going to order his inner environment—his thoughts, his feelings, his being. No matter how much they took from him—which was every person and material thing he had—he still had this freedom—the freedom to choose.[20]

Like Dr. Frankl, we have the freedom to choose also. We cannot always choose what happens to us, but we can always choose our reaction to what comes into our life. We can, like Dr. Frankl, choose to let go of the heartache.

Holding onto hurt is like binding the victim to the perpetrator with invisible chains. The victim holds in his hands the hurt that he has had in his heart. Attached to one end of that hurt is the offender. His offense gives him a hold on the victim's heart. Every time there is a reminder of that hurt, the victim feels a tug on his heart that dredges up the past agonies. Forgiving means every time the victim feels a tug of remembrance, he gives some small part of that agony to Jesus. As he is reminded by some outside stimuli, he feels the gentle tug of Jesus.

> "I can forgive, but I cannot forget," is only another way of saying, "I will not forgive." Forgiveness ought to be like a cancelled note— torn in two, and burned up, so that it can never be shown against one."
> –Henry Beecher Ward

Forgiveness is: He tugs, I give. He tugs, I give. He tugs, I give. He tugs, I give, and one day, I say, "I believe I will be all right."

> Does Jesus care when my heart is pained
> Too deeply for mirth and song;
> As the burdens press, and the cares distress,
> And the way grows weary and long:

> Does Jesus care when my way is dark
> With a nameless dread and fear?
> As the daylights fades into deep night shades,
> Does He care enough to be near?

Does Jesus care when I've tried and failed
To resist some temptation strong;
When for my deep grief I find no relief,
Tho' my tears flow all the night long?

Does Jesus care when I've said "good-by"
To the dearest on earth to me,
And my sad heart aches till it nearly breaks—
Is it aught to Him? Does He see?

O yes, He cares; I know He cares;
His heart is touched with my grief;
When the days are weary, the long nights dreary,
I know my Saviour cares.

CHAPTER TWO

Trying to Smooth Out the Ripples of My Life

Prerequisite Reading
Luke 15:11-32

When I began to present this series to the members of the First Baptist Church of Hammond, I received more letters in one week than after any sermon I have ever preached. I felt like my words touched the hearts of many hurting people. It seemed as though I had touched a sensitive nerve that caused excruciating pain—like cold water running over a tooth with an exposed nerve ending. I sensed I had opened up partially healed wounds. Some people made statements like, "Your words opened wounds that I believed had been successfully bottled up for good."

Others said, "For the first time in my life, you explained why I was struggling in a certain area. No book or tract or pamphlet or sermon that I could find addressed my issues."

Though I do not make my pulpit a psychiatrist's couch, I do want to help those who constantly struggle with issues from the past. Some men of God preach and teach that the grace of God can take care of any problem as if to say that whatever is in your past is simply forgiven, forgotten, and bears no repercussions in your present or future life. On the other hand, the same preachers hold a teen meeting and proceed to breathe out God's wrath at the young people saying, "If you don't behave yourself, you'll bear the scars of these sins all the days of your life."

Every person wants to know which view is right! These paradoxical statements illicit an explanation. Suppose a person lives a life of debauchery and sin, of wantonness and waste, and ruin. Suppose he trashes all the good that has been given to him on the altar of selfishness, self-will, pride, arrogance, impudence, and rebellion. Does his behavior have any bearing on his future or his children's future?

What exactly would you like preachers to tell their young people and children? Do we tell the young people, "It doesn't really matter how you live because after you turn 25 or 30 and decide to turn your life around, you can just forget about the years of sin. So what if you wasted many good years! So what if you brought the evil spirits of debauchery into your life. So what if you made cocaine, liquor, and cigarettes a part of your life."

Is wine a mocker as Proverbs 20:1 says it is, or is it not? *"Wine is a mocker, strong drink is raging: and whosoever is deceived thereby is not wise."* Does indulging in alcoholic beverages have any bearing upon your present or future? Since your sins are forgiven, are there any repercussions on the lives of other people who have to live with your decisions?

I often tell the Hyles-Anderson College students, "If you want to know what one decision and its cause-and-effect relationship have, take a 40-pound cement block to Beverly Island in the middle of the beautiful five-acre lake on our campus, get as close to the water as you can, and heave that cement block into the water. Only one big splash will take place because that block will promptly sink to the bottom of the lake. After a while the surface grows placid. However, if you watch carefully, and especially if the lake is smooth, the ripples will start fanning out from the initial splash. Eventually, you will notice that the ripples touch all of the shoreline around the entire lake—one splash equals perennial ripples. The first splash is the biggest, but the ripples continue for a long time after the initial impact. In other words, your one decision will touch the lives of many."

Every teenager has to live his life. The one who decides to flaunt the rules and indulge in rule-breaking activities probably won't immediately feel the hand of God because our God is a much more merciful God than anyone could ever imagine. Many times God doesn't pay off the premiums immediately. The farmer who sows his corn in May does not reap his crop in June; he picks the corn in November.

> Are you loaded down with regrets and mistakes? Remorse is futile worry and self-inflicted agony for some yesterday.
> –Unknown

Tragically, those who do not get punished immediately start thinking, "I got by with my sin!" Some of them even graduate from a good, solid Bible college. Some enjoy sharing their stories of misconduct and brag, "We never got caught! Nothing happened to us! We didn't get killed! We even graduated!" Believe it or not, some even graduate with honors. An even more tragic scenario is the effect the rule breakers have on those who follow the rules. As they watch what did **not** happen, they start thinking, "They sinned, and they got by with it. I believe I can too!"

Is the man of God preaching truth when he says, "If you choose to make that splash of sin in your life, does it or does it not have a ripple effect through the ages of your life"? Is the Bible accurate when it says that God visits the iniquity of the father on his children to the third and fourth generation? "...*forgiving iniquity and transgression and sin, and that will by no means clear the guilty; visiting the iniquity of the fathers upon the children, and upon the children's children, unto the third and to the fourth generation.*"

(Exodus 34:7) The Bible does not say the third and fourth generation of family members have to commit the same sins.

Do you believe that because the ripples gradually smooth out that they have little or no effect? It is very important for believers to reconcile these two concepts. Not understanding these two concepts is a large reason why so many of God's people struggle while trying to grow in the Christian life. For example, a son feels he is the result of the rippled effect of a dad who terribly mishandled him. The son might well consider that perhaps his father's mishandling of him was the providence of God.

After preaching one Sunday night on the inner hurts, the very first letter I opened the following day was as follows:

"Dear Brother Schaap,

I'm fourteen and a half years old. I've been raped—many, many times by a brother and a father. My mother refuses to do anything about it, except we weep together.

Can you please meet with me? Can you please have somebody talk to me? I cut myself all of the time. I hurt myself regularly trying to hurt the persons who hurt me."

To be sure, your personal difficulties may not be as severe as this young lady's problems, or they may possibly be more severe. I could share many illustrations of people who seek counsel and tell me about the hurt they feel from people who have wounded them. What began as "a splash in the pond" of their life keeps rippling to all the shorelines of their emotions.

When a man of God says, "The grace of God can take away your past," the wounds of someone who is injured often remain coiled like a tightly wound spring deep within him. The anger and bitterness often abide within even as the person begs, "God, I know You forgave me of my sins, but how do I deal with the ripple effect of all of the sin and the hurt of those who have brought shame and agony into my life?"

The very familiar story of the prodigal son is a story of healing for hurting hearts. These conflicting issues are addressed in the story of the prodigal son which focuses on two brothers and a father.

1. The Injury. *"And the younger of them said to his father, Father, give me the portion of goods that falleth to me. And he divided unto them his living. And not many days after the younger son gathered all together, and took his journey into a far country, and there wasted his substance with riotous living."* (Luke 15:12, 13) I am sure this parable causes many people to wonder why God does not step in and stop people from making foolish choices.

Shortly after the tragedy of the Twin Towers on September 11, 2001, so often a person echoed the sentiments of many others as he asked me, "Why didn't God stop that from happening?"

Basically I answered in the same way every time I was asked, "Why?" I offered, "Why didn't He stop the holocaust from happening? Why didn't He stop the rape of Nanking when tens of thousands of Chinese were destroyed by the Japanese? Why did He not stop the pillaging of the Philippines by the Americans in the early 1900s, a horrific event recorded in history as a great victory? Why didn't He stop soldiers from killing every child under the age of ten in the Philippines? Why didn't He step in and stop American frontiersmen from slaughtering Indian people?" Many stories which are

> One thing we may be sure of: For the believer, all pain has meaning; all adversity is profitable. There is no question that adversity is difficult. It usually takes us by surprise and seems to strike where we are most vulnerable. To us, it often appears senseless and irrational, but to God none of it is either senseless or irrational. He has a purpose in every pain He brings or allows in our lives. We can be sure that in some way He intends it for our profit and His glory.
> –Jerry Bridges

absolutely gruesome and vicious propagandize how the Indians were the "bad guys." Could He not have stopped the sinking of the H.M.S. *Titanic?* Could He not have stopped two space shuttles from exploding? Could He not have stopped the murdering and the pillaging of Iraq under the reign of Saddam Hussein? Of course He could have stopped these events and every other heinous crime committed in all of time!

I added, "What we are witnessing is not the impotence of God; instead, we are watching the free will of man. God decided that He would let every human being decide what to do with his life. God decided to let me make my decisions as to what I would do with my life. Do you want anyone dictating to you how to live your life?"

This great doctrine of the free will of man inspired John Bunyan, John Locke, and even Thomas Jefferson as he framed the Declaration of Independence. The free will of man is the foundation of the American legal system which guarantees our individual liberties that are granted by God—not by religions or governments. John Bunyan wrote, "Rights granted to men by men may be denied by men, rights granted to men by God can only be denied by God." No red-blooded American man wants anyone telling him what to do! God, in His kindness, made a decision not to divorce Himself from us. He allows us to make free-will choices. We are spectators watching on a daily basis the free exercise of the free will of mankind.

The prodigal's father did not stop his younger son from leaving home and destroying his life through debauchery. In somewhat the same respect, nobody stops another human being from trusting Christ as his Saviour. Nobody stops the rebel from going to a strip club or from smoking his first marijuana cigarette. No one could stop 7,000 teenagers in America from losing their virginity in any one calendar day.

God allows mankind to have a free will. He could have

stopped Eve from taking and eating the fruit, but He chose to allow man to freely make his moral decisions. I thank God He does, but doing so was a tremendous risk. At times that risk exceeds the favor of discretion.

I meet many young people who are the victims of someone who used his free moral agency to prey upon that young person when he was too young to prevent the abuse from happening. That injury is indicative of someone who wants to exercise his freedom and take another's from him. Free moral agency is when someone exercises his freedom of sensual pleasure and robs a little girl of her innocence. The same question, from saved and unsaved alike, always follows: "God, why didn't You step in and stop it?"

Do you really want God to stop you every time you make a decision? Before becoming too pharisaical and hypocritical about people who exercise and abuse their free will agency, keep in mind that every single one of us exercises our free moral agency every single day. Some of us choose to cheat on our taxes; others choose to cheat God and withhold their tithe.

Let's say that a person's free moral agency ends with his ability to choose whether or not to give tithes and offerings. Suppose he decides not to tithe because he has his family vacation coming; he has just prostituted God's money. Do we really want God to dictate to us so we have no choice in the matter of paying our tithes and offerings? I, for one, don't! I want God to risk trusting me. I say to the Almighty, "God, I can't believe You would trust me!"

If I could have been a time traveler and was invited to sit on a committee about free will and choices, I might well have said, "God, maybe You don't really want to do that. You will open a door for mankind to murder and pillage. You will see a Chicago teenager murdered in 2005 for a pair of $115 sneakers."

Those kinds of incidents happen when we want to exercise our rights and tell people how to run their life. We want to put our foot down, but we don't want God putting His foot down until we get injured. We say, "God, I want to make *my* own choices," until we get injured!

Behind every flaw in human character is an injury caused by sin and pride. Every person has a besetting sin—the result of a wound that doesn't heal properly. There is a difference between a wound and a scar. A scar is a reminder of an injury that healed properly. For instance, I have a two-inch long scar on my wrist. When I was a six-year-old boy, I was so eager to play with my buddies that I put my hand through a glass door. As I ran up to my grandparents' house, I missed the little lever that opened the glass door. That scar still remains as a reminder to be careful.

I also have an almost unnoticeable scar on my forehead. As a child I was standing on the transmission "hump" so I could see out the window, and Dad suddenly slammed on the brakes. Before he could throw out his arm to catch me, I slammed my head into the dashboard of the car. Just as we receive physical injuries that leave physical scars, we also receive spiritual and emotional injuries that leave inward scars. Many times those injuries become excuses for why we do wrong.

I have reiterated oftentimes that **the hero is someone who succeeds while struggling with the same problems losers use as an excuse for failure.** Anyone who wants an excuse can probably find an injury in his past. More than likely, he can find some prodigal who hurt his feelings, wounded his emotions, trampled on his feelings, made fun of him, picked on him, humiliated him, rejected him, and ostracized him from the "in" crowd. The person can hide behind that episode and use that as an excuse to sow his wild oats. Their supposed injury produces weeds in the gardens of marriage, in successive generations, and in the work place. Be careful about saying, "I'm going to test what it is like out there." There are already enough injuries to hide behind without turning to sin.

Parents, take heed! When your children graduate from high school, please "sit on them" harder than you have ever before sat on them. Ride herd on them like you have never before ridden herd on them. Being eighteen and graduated is meaningless! Eighteen is simply a number that follows seventeen, and graduation simply means they go off to college.

Parents, don't let a high-school graduate talk you into something you know is wrong by his saying, "Well, I'm 18 years old."

If he tries that tactic, just calmly reply, "I'm 47, and I can count as high as you can and even a little higher."

If your high-school graduate has a problem with your being the head of the house and the one who is in charge, then give him a good reason why he does not want to misbehave! Don't sit by idly when a teenage boy (or girl) graduates from high school and states, "I'm 18; I'll do what my friends say!"

Parents, that house is still your house. Tell him he will do what you tell him to do. Tell him he will be in by the normal curfew or else! Too many parents become spineless weaklings as parents just because Junior is 18, has graduated from high school, and has grown taller than his parents. Don't lose courage from all the times you said, "Be home when I tell you to be home," and he was home. It's time for a revival of moms and dads who watch their young people and children. Surely you do not want them sowing their wild oats and trashing their lives! **Youthful indulgences bring family wounds that often bleed for three and four generations.**

College-age young adults, high school graduates, and college graduates who are still single often feel left out, and as a result, they are trying to find themselves. In trying to "find themselves," far too many make unwise decisions to indulge in watching HBO movies, trying liquor, and stepping outside the boundaries of decent and proper dating behavior to the realm of acting like married couples without the license. May I warn you that the iniquity you are committing will be visited to your children, to your grandchildren, and to your great-grandchildren? *"...for I the LORD thy God am a jealous God, visiting the iniquity of the fathers upon the children unto the third and fourth generation of them that hate me."* (Deuteronomy 5:9) Your shallow excuse of "finding yourself" will have a ripple effect. Young adult, behave yourself because you have no idea how many ripples you will create by one singular decision. How do I know? An injury took place when the prodigal son said, "I believe I will test the waters! I want to examine them for myself and test the validity of my father's admonitions." Your father's admonitions are based on wisdom and experience. I would take good heed to what my father says because experience is not the best teacher; someone else's experience is!

   2. The Injustice. *"And he arose, and came to his father. But when he was yet a great way off, his father saw him, and had compassion, and ran, and fell on his neck, and kissed him. And the son said unto him, Father, I have sinned against heaven, and in thy sight, and am no more worthy to be called thy son. But the father said to his servants, Bring forth the best robe, and put it on him; and put a ring on his hand, and shoes on his feet: And bring hither the fatted calf, and kill it; and let us eat, and be merry: For this my son was dead, and is alive again; he was lost, and is found. And they began to be merry."* (Luke 15:20-24)
   Like the prodigal son of Luke 15, some profligate everything they receive and prostitute every decent thing in their lives. Unholiness was the walk of their licentious living, wicked behavior, fornication, debauchery, drunkenness, and drugs. Hopefully, those who choose this path with perversion will eventually come to their senses, like the prodigal who came to himself. As the prodigal pondered his desperate straits, he thought of home. "My father's servants live better than I do. I will go home to my father and say, 'Father, I have sinned and am not worthy to be called your son.' " One wanders from the narrow path, comes to church, and for the first time in a long time, makes his way to the altar and

finds a Father Who says, "I forgive you."

On behalf of those of who are not and never have been prodigals, that hurts! The prodigal's older brother hurt! "Why?" the prodigal asks.

The brother hurts because the one who did not do the wrong felt the sting of his younger brother's sin. When the prodigal left home, the honorable brother's work load doubled! When the prodigal escaped from the confines of his home, his older brother was reminded every day not to break his mother's heart like his brother did. He probably heard a sermon every day from his mother about not breaking his father's heart. He had to bear his parents' deep sorrow.

Then the elder brother watched his young brother return to a festive welcome. It was like nothing had ever happened. He was probably shocked by the rejoicing. "He's home! He's home! Our son is home!"

The honorable brother was probably thinking, "It's about time, you reprobate! The whole time you were gone I had to hear about how you shamed our name. I had to go to church and school and face your friends. I had to make excuses about where you were. I had to cover for your reprehensible character. I had to listen to our parents grieve over you."

Thank God for all those who didn't take the prodigal's path. But an injustice takes place when the prodigal comes home, and suddenly it's party time. The preacher leaves the pulpit to welcome the prodigal son with open arms, while the honorable son watches and thinks, "The pastor never went out of his way to hug me when I came to church. He never went out of his way to thank me for being good."

A deep and powerful injury takes place. The righteous kid says, "Hearing all that sermonizing from the pulpit, hearing my parents' constant admonition, hearing the weeping of my mother through the long nights, and listening to our father trying to comfort her was because of your choice, not mine! You came home; you are given a welcome-home party; you have the pastor's affection, and you are being praised for coming home! The preacher said that sin does not pay. To me, it looks like it's paying some really good dividends."

The prodigal tries to justify his party and his welcome with statements like, "You haven't had the pigpen's life!"

"No, my prodigal brother, I haven't had a pigpen's life. May I remind you—you chose it!" When the prodigal chose his life of sin, his behavior had a ripple effect on many others.

Several times I have met with men who have lost their ministry, and all they want is to bemoan their loss and have back what they lost. The typical stance and statement I hear is, "I don't understand why people won't forgive me. Where is the grace and forgiveness of Christians?"

What happened to their righteousness and good choices? Some of these men preached for years about reading the Bible and praying, but when they made the choice to dispense with these things, all they want is forgiveness. They want to have a big Band-aid applied to the wound and to hear some soothing words like, "We're so sorry for you! It surely did hurt to live in sin, didn't it?"

What happened to good choices when you freely and deliberately chose to make some incredibly stupid decisions that have robbed you of everything good in life, especially your reputation and your testimony? The result of your exodus into worldly living is to whine about how hard it was for you! What happened to good choices?!

"Don't even try to cry on my shoulder," the elder brother says. "I had to stay home and listen to our mother cry night after night. I had to listen our mother praying and asking God, 'Where's my boy?' I wanted to go into her room and say, 'I'm right here!' but I wasn't good enough because she couldn't have you!"

An injury always accompanies sin. When the prodigal sinned,

he caused a ripple effect that injured everyone whose life he touched. The father was caught in the middle trying to placate a son and begging them both to get along. More than likely, the two brothers never did.

A terrible injustice also took place. The elder brother watched his younger brother's wrongdoing be forgiven and forgotten by those who threatened and warned him not to embrace sin, when he had made a conscious choice to ignore their warnings. When an honorable son has to watch a prodigal enjoy the limelight, he might well begin thinking, "Why shouldn't I go live in sin? Why shouldn't I live a life of debauchery like my brother? After all, when I decide to come home, the family will have a party, people will tell me how wonderful it is to have me home, and I'll get a diamond ring and some new clothes. That sounds like a good deal to me. I get to have my sin and be rewarded with a welcome-home party."

The story of the prodigal son illustrates the injustice of sin. Grace and forgiveness always appear to be a "cheap" way to handle the person who didn't do right. Seemingly, the wicked son was exalted, and the honorable son was scolded.

3. The Insult. *"And he was angry, and would not go in: therefore came his father out, and intreated him. And he answering said to his father, Lo, these many years do I serve thee, neither transgressed I at any time thy commandment: and yet thou never gavest me a kid, that I might make merry with my friends: But as soon as this thy son was come, which hath devoured thy living with harlots, thou hast killed for him the fatted calf."* (Luke 15:28-30) Righteous indignation filled the soul of the honorable son.

He was saying to his father, "I obeyed your commandments. I went to work every day, Dad. I did not cause you any problems. You are angry at me because I can't deal with the fact that my brother trashed our family's name and our feelings. Because I am defending you, you are angry at me?"

This firm father appears weak, unjust, and inconsistent. The bad boy never got punished. I believe the elder son could have handled his brother's return so much better if his father would have said, "Glad you're home," and then punished him. Possibly the prodigal would have asked his brother for forgiveness too. I believe the older brother had every right to be upset. I find it amazing how people so easily justify their sins. I've heard all kinds of faulty reasoning like, "I was young and foolish," or "I didn't know what I was talking about."

When I was the vice-president at Hyles-Anderson College, one of my duties was overseeing the discipline at the college. I was in a meeting with a young man who was being expelled, and he said to me, "Brother Schaap, I don't understand why you are expelling me! All I did was go to a restaurant and drink some beer. Now, you are kicking me out of school! Don't tell me that when you were 19, you wouldn't have tried some!"

"I **was** 19," I said, "and I did **NOT** take it! We were both tempted, son! The difference is that I realized when I was 19 what a ripple effect I would cause if I did something so stupid as to try drinking!"

People do not like their punishment because it exposes their stupidity. Everyone who sins wants to cry, "Where's the forgiveness?" The injury and injustice and then the insult—the pain of doing right and being scolded for it—because he was not kind to his prodigal brother, was a wound that deeply hurt the honorable son. Hopefully these thoughts will help some people who wonder why they struggle when a friend or a family member wounded their loved ones. They suffer with an injustice and deep insult.

"And he [the father] *said unto him, Son, thou art ever with me, and all that I have is thine. It was meet* [or necessary] *that we should make merry, and be glad: for this thy brother was dead, and is alive again; and was lost, and is found."* (Luke 15:31, 32) I am trying to help us see the other side of the story. Jesus reconciles the story as

the father praises his honorable son and invites him to come to the party.

4. The Invitation. I would like to address the story of the prodigal son from yet a different point of view. I believe my perspective will not do any disservice to the Scriptures. Though I cannot prove this, to me, in some respects, the elder son represents God the Father.

In about 20 passages in the Old Testament, God had to "bite His tongue" and hold His peace, while His wrath boiled inside of Him. He kept the anger, wrath, and hurt pent up inside of Him through 4,000 years until Jesus Christ died on the cross. Holy is the Lord, and we tend to forget that the wrath of the Lord God was kindled greatly over and over again. Time and again God was ready to slaughter His chosen people for their insults and making a mockery of every good thing He had done!

Our God is a consuming fire. Imagine all the years of wrath He suppressed as He watched His chosen people fall into Baal worship and bow down to idols. The grinding of that terrible hurt was what the Elder Son felt! Calvary was God taking 4,000 years of insult, and an explosion of anger and wrath was vented on the Son of God! Every time God had had to restrain His anger, it was unleashed at the cross; and Jesus was pierced, wounded, beaten, insulted, ridiculed, and rejected for God. Calvary was for God to be vindicated.

Calvary was for every insult, and every injury, and every injustice to every human who ever lived. On the cross, Jesus said to His Father, "Let go of every insult You have borne, every shame You have suffered, every rejection You have felt, every proud and haughty look aimed at You, every act of intimidation against You, every affront, every accusation, every scolding You received for doing right, every filthy lie that was told about You, and every filthy word that was used against You!" God turned His face from His own Son as He realized He had to let it go.

To me, the story of the prodigal was Jesus Christ making His Father look good! To me, Jesus was saying, "For 4,000 years I have lived with My Father in Heaven, and I've seen My Father hurt for 4,000 years. I have heard My Father wonder why He made man. I have heard My Father's voice thunder across Heaven saying, 'Why? Why don't they love Me? Why do they reject Me? Why don't they want Me?' " Jesus came to earth to die on a cross to make His Father look good!

I cannot adequately explain it, but when Jesus hung on that cross, every hurt anyone has ever felt, He felt. Every hurt His Father felt, He felt. To every pain that God could feel and every pain that man could feel, Jesus said, "Let it go. Can you let it all go for My sake?"

You must go to the foot of the cross, look at that Saviour, and say, "For Jesus' sake, I'll let go of the injury, the insult, and the injustice because that is the only hope I have." If you do not forgive, those ripples will just keep on slamming into each successive generation. You will never ever fix the injury until you go to the cross and see the One Who took your injury. "Father, let it go."

CHAPTER THREE

Jesus, the Friend
of a Wounded Heart

Prerequisite Reading
Hebrews 12:1-3

In our journey of life, we humans tend to pick up an enormous amount of baggage. Our emotional baggage tends to stay with us through life and weigh us down until, at some point, the baggage becomes more than we can humanly lift and handle. We find ourselves emotionally buckling under many responsibilities like marriage and other important relationships. People in their mid-forties and early fifties label this time of life "mid-life burnout" or "mid-life crisis."

I receive many letters from people my age who ask, "How do you handle the burnout you must be feeling from the ministry?"

Truthfully, I don't feel burned out! I feel like I possess an impatient expectancy, an eagerness to go forward, and a desire to light the world on fire. *Feeling* pressured is another story! I feel like I am in the grips of an emotional vice almost every day of my life. Sometimes, I almost feel as though the weight of the world rests on my shoulders—especially after several counseling sessions in a row.

A pastor said to me recently, "I just don't know how I can take any more. I am pastoring about 75 people, and I am just flat burned out. Do you have any idea what I'm feeling?"

"No, I don't," I admitted. "I've never pastored a church of 75; 10,000 or 12,000 maybe, but not 75. Perhaps it is much tougher to pastor 75 people." I thought, "It must be easy to pastor a large church because there are no problems!"

For the most part, I enjoy working with people, and I am glad to help these people with their baggage. I love to counsel our people and meet with them. I use their stories for chapel and for sermon illustrations! Seriously, I hurt for so many people who carry a load of emotional baggage they cannot seem to shed. They remind me of John Bunyan's *Pilgrim's Progress*—a great book every Christian should read.

In a nutshell, the story unfolds about a young man named Pilgrim traveling on his journey through the Christian life. He carries a great weight and baggage on his shoulder which he slowly learns to release, let fall off, and it tumbles down a hill. Of course, he feels an immense relief from having that great weight lifted off of his shoulders.

In the same way, my desire is to help other Christians to shed some of the baggage they feel they must carry. Regrettably, this baggage comes from a variety of sources—especially the sins of our youth. We dabble in "experimental" sins and fail to realize that every time we open up a door to some sin, that door never seems to shut properly again.

Thinking about that opened door makes me think of my car. I have the feeling that some people must hate my car because it is in the shop for the fourth time in less than a year! I just got it out of the shop from being rear-ended for the third time! Please have mercy on my car! Three people have already taken turns telling me what they do not like about my car, and now a fourth person has decided to make a statement about my car. He broadsided my car, and now the driver's door doesn't work very well. As I drive the car, the wind whistles in through the dent. In order to get the door shut, I have to slam it. If I slam the front door so it shuts semi-properly, the back door won't open at all! Mine is a "wonderful" predicament.

I feel like my car problems are a picture of some people's lives. When we fix one problem, another one opens or another one shuts. Experimenting with sins is like having your car broadsided or rear ended! Damage has been done that can never fully be undone. I encourage mothers and fathers to keep their children innocent and naive and keep them from experimenting with sin. Don't let sin become an accessible opportunity for satisfying curiosity.

When Losses Come

How do you make up for the pain of loss? Suppose a parent is taken prematurely. No human being can ever take the place of a father. A young boy or a young girl feels an incredible, indescribable pain at the loss of either parent. That young person could easily buckle under from that pain and want to run away, but there's nowhere to run. Who can you tell what it's like to lose a father or a mother at a young age?

Hurt is so real in this life we live. Many times the emotions feel like nerves which are stretched and taut and on edge. Another person's careless look, an indiscriminate comment, an insult in the classroom about your weight or your size, or some calloused words like "You won't understand because you don't have a dad," impact so deeply that the person feels like he can barely stagger through life. He must plaster what I call "a plastic look on his face" and act like a tough guy or a tough girl to survive. As a result, more baggage is added to the already excessive, oppressive bundle he is trying to carry.

A spouse dies, and that dreaded appellation "widow" or "widower" is attached to your name. Nobody wants that label attached to his or her life. The one group of people that I labor hard to try to help and that I feel so absolutely helpless in doing so is that precious group of people called widows and widowers. The intense loneliness they feel and the emptiness and void they confront daily is very real, very profound, and very powerful.

Emotional hurts create intense loneliness and feelings of deep insecurity and fear. The loss of a parent, a spouse, or a child creates a vacuum of profound, intense insecurity. With that vacuity comes the fear of being rejected and the fear of being left alone again. The person craves security and desires to have everything restored to what it was before the loss of the loved one. Having that missing puzzle piece to restore the picture properly and wholly becomes the singular goal of the hurting one. However, life seemingly does nothing but remind you that it can never go back to what it was before. You feel like God Himself is insulting you. So, you make statements like, "Why would God do that to me? Why does God hate me so much?"

When a child is violated by a predator, innocence is lost—never to be regained. "Feelings of shame, guilt, and self-blame are common following a sexual assault. Individuals often report a feeling of shame for having been sexually assaulted as well as a sense of shame about their perceived responsibility for the assault."[1]

As many as half of all those who have been assaulted have symptoms of a major depression soon after the assault. Tearfulness, sadness, poor concentration, loss of interest and enjoyment in normal activities and relationships are all commonly experienced after an assault. In addition, the following difficulties should be assessed: sleep disturbance (typically early waking), appetite change, weight loss, diurnal variation of mood, psychomotor retardation or agitation, feelings of guilt, worthlessness, and suicidal thoughts."[2]

A spouse's perfidy seems to cheapen the marriage vows. As a result, the marriage ends, parents divorce, and tough-acting children, who put on a strong emotional veneer, feel an emotional abyss of betrayal. "How could Mom and Dad say they love us and do this to us?" The children naturally gravitate toward feeling guilty and thinking somehow it is all their fault. Their hidden hurt is so real. Who dries the tears that children and teens weep privately? To whom do they turn when they feel there's not a human being left in the world to trust?

These emotional hurts create intense insecurity and fear—feelings we just don't know what to do with. In our loneliness and fear, we seek approval and acceptance, begging for someone to say, "I love you" and "I like you just the way you are."

I cannot help but think of a former assistant pastor from First Baptist Church of Hammond who had never heard the words "I love you" until he heard them from the girl he would eventually marry. He heard the words a second time when visiting First Baptist Church and hearing Brother Hyles say, "I love you, C.W."

People with incredible hurts are searching for someone to say, "I love you, and I believe in you." Because of that incredible desire to hear we are loved, far too often we seek approval and acceptance in all the wrong places.

Teenagers especially have an intense need to be accepted. Before I became pastor of First Baptist Church of Hammond, I often spoke at youth meetings—as many as 35 a year. Often the host pastor would meet with me prior to the service and would say something like, "Brother Schaap, we have some good church kids hanging around with the wrong crowd. Please address that issue."

I always wanted to say to the pastor, "Do you really know what the wrong crowd is?" I believe the wrong crowd is the one crowd that will accept a kid for what he is. They may teach him all the wrong things, but that kid is desperately searching for someone who likes him just the way he is without judging him. The wrong crowd doesn't care how a new "inductee" wears his hair, how he looks, or what music he enjoys. They welcome him into their group because they too are looking for someone who likes them just the way they are.

When some guest preacher says, "You have to separate yourself from a certain type of of kids," they automatically think, "No way! That's the only crowd that accepts me! They let me speak my mind or say nothing; I am still accepted by them. I ran to this crowd because they are the only people who like me just the way I am. They fill the void in my life."

So often these young people gravitate toward the world as they follow the crowd who "accepts" them. One very famous rock 'n' roller who died years ago, Jimi Hendrix, said, "Rock 'n' roll fills the hole in your soul."

I disagree with Jimi! A void may be filled, but rock music does not fill it full, and it doesn't fill it to satisfying. Only Jesus can satisfy your soul! Fulfillment will not come by looking in all the wrong places for all the wrong things.

In my late twenties, I went through some struggles of wondering about my life. Even a Christian can reach a bottom point in his life when he starts wondering whether or not life is worth living. Perhaps he even starts fingering the trigger of a gun, wondering if maybe a bullet is the best way to end it all. When a person reaches that low point, he stops wondering why people turn to alcohol, or to drugs, or to wicked music that teaches some very negative concepts. Turning to worldly activities becomes a way to escape the pain in his heart. Because I went through some times of baffling hurts, I believe I can understand to some extent why a Christian might turn to those places to satisfy a hurt in his heart that seemingly won't go away. A lonely person reaches for that which often becomes the baggage he cannot be rid of later in life. Besetting sins are those negative actions and negatives attitudes to which a person turns when he feels hurt or rejected. What a person turns to when he feels rejected by someone usually becomes a weight or a besetting sin.

When the Bible says we should "lay aside every weight and the sin which so easily besets us," the Bible doesn't say that we can be forever rid of that weight. The Bible does not use language like, "*Forever* rid yourself of it." Rather, the Word of God says, "Lay it aside!" In Hebrews 12:1, 2, the Bible commands the Christian to "lay them aside." He cannot permanently remove them because they have become too much a part of the fabric of his life. Thankfully, we can cast them aside! That wording is very important for a person in understanding how to have victory in his Christian life.

No doubt you have watched an NBA basketball game, and the coach sends in another player. When that player waits on the bench, he is generally dressed in "warmups." The moment the coach calls his name and signals him to enter the game, the player stands, rips off his warmups, and throws them aside. He goes into the game and plays. As long as he is in that game, the warmups have been cast aside. When he leaves the game for any length of time, the first thing he generally does is put on his warmups again. When playing the game—running his race, if you please—he puts aside the weight of his warmups to improve his playing ability.

A besetting sin can be what one wears to give him a feeling of security. A besetting sin can be what one wears when he is not in the game—perhaps because of injury. Even though you cannot play in the game, you are still wearing warmups and sitting on the bench. The writer, the Apostle Paul, uses a race—much like a jogging course and says, "You can't run a race wearing warmups! Get them off, get in the race, and don't stop running."

As long as you are actively involved in trying to help your team win that game or in helping the coach with the running of the plays or in helping your fans bring home a victory, you don't need to carry the weight of that besetting sin. However, as soon as you get out of the game, that is exactly when you run to the security of those weights and besetting sins. How very important it is to **stay** in the game!

Whenever a baseball pitcher is pitching and returns to the dugout from the pitching area, he often puts on a jacket to protect his pitching arm. Just before he warms up, he takes off the jacket to throw several pitches, and then he starts pitching the game. As soon as he returns to the dugout, he puts his jacket back on because that jacket gives him a sense of security and warmth for that throwing shoulder.

What the writer is saying is that if you are pitching the game—if you are staying in the game—take off that jacket; lay it aside! You don't need that extra weight. He says, "You can never get rid of it permanently because your life has been built too much around it, but if you'll stay in the game, you won't need it permanently."

Perhaps life has dealt you some unexpected twists and turns, and you have reached for things such as cigarettes or liquor or negative music or pornography or illicit affairs or adultery—besetting sins. These private, secret sins are sins about which only you and God know, and you have turned to these sins because of the debilitating wound that occurred in your life. That wound upsets your emotions and hurts so deeply you don't know what to do.

When I was growing up in Holland, Michigan, we lived close to a very busy street. When I was a junior-aged lad, I loved to watch my uncle, Lloyd Schaap, drive a Kenworth diesel gravel truck that hauled 80,000 pounds of gravel. He would drive by my house several times a day going back and forth from the gravel pit to the place where he was dropping it off. We would wave at each other. Sometimes he would honk the horn, pull over, and stop. When he wanted me to ride along, he would honk the horn, and that was our signal for me to get permission to go with him. I would quickly get permission to go, run out to where he was parked, climb up, open the door, and ride in that big truck with him for several hours. One day I saw him coming down the road, and he honked the horn. I waved at my uncle and ran inside the house to ask my parents if I could ride with Uncle Lloyd.

This particular time, I was so eager to go with my uncle that I lunged for the long handle alongside the door, but I missed it. Right next to the handle was the unprotected smokestack which was several hundred degrees hot. As I reached for the handle, I was already looking inside the window, and I accidentally grabbed the smokestack. Almost instantly my hand seared to the smokestack. My system was so shocked by the unexpected contact that I couldn't pull away. The pain was so excruciating, I couldn't even choke out the word, "Help." I could feel the panic rising within me—just like a silent scream.

My dad had walked out of the house to make sure I got to the truck. He realized what happened, and he ran as fast as he could toward the truck. My uncle was puzzled by what was happening, so he climbed out of his truck to investigate. He suddenly saw my hand on the smokestack and realized that I could not let go. My flesh was burning from the excessive heat. My dad reached me before my uncle, and he grabbed my wrist and pulled my hand free. I remember that day vividly and how the pain was indescribable. I remember that my hand hurt so badly I could not form words. I couldn't even cry for a while.

Just like I mistakenly grabbed that hot smokestack, some of you have reached for the wrong things in life, and you added insult to injury when you made that unwise decision. You didn't intend to hurt yourself, but the pain of your lonely heart grabbed something that burned you. You desperately wish someone could come and rescue you from that which is doing nothing to bring you a better life and pour healing ointment on the wounds. Someone will; His name is Jesus Christ! He would like to rescue you, pour the balm of Gilead on your injuries, and minister healing to you.

Thankfully, my hand healed, and I did not suffer any ill effects from my mistake. Obviously, I learned from my mistakes, and I do not have a besetting habit of grabbing hot smokestacks. Obviously, nobody would get in the habit of grabbing smokestacks like I did as a child; but even in First Baptist Church of Hammond, hundreds of people have habits that are hurting more than that smokestack burn hurt me. They reach for those devastating habits, and these practices either hurt them physically or re-injure them emotionally, or set a trap for them. When the person becomes older, these habits will continue to bring more pain, more ruin, and more devastation.

May I say to you that Jesus Christ would like to rescue you from that which would hurt you so deeply! You should consider giving Jesus Christ your heartaches because He understands. Jesus Christ went to a cross.

What do I mean? As a young 33-year-old strong, masculine man, Jesus knew that He was going to die a despicable death—not the kind of death reserved for kings and nobles like He was. Rather, to His shame, His was the death reserved for thieves and murderers, liars and cheats, one reserved for traitors and for those who commit treason. His was a death befitting predators and violators and reserved for those who were the wicked off-scouring of society. Jesus despised that shame! He did not even care about that shame!

Why? Because the Bible says He endured the cross. "Enduring the cross" does not mean "I've got to go through this!" or "I must endure" like a student taking a final exam or a standardized test. No! Jesus went to the cross having made the decision to go through the full measure of the cross, deciding to stay on that cross until everything that He went to the cross to do had been accomplished.

He went to the cross to die for our sins, to pay our sin penalty, and to shed a holy God's blood so He could pay for the transgression of our sins. But He had to go to the cross for yet another reason. *"For we have not an high priest which cannot be touched with the feeling of our infirmities; but was in all points tempted like as we are, yet without sin."* (Hebrews 4:15) Jesus went to the cross because He wanted every hurting human heart to know that there is one Person Who deeply feels exactly the way they feel. Jesus wanted to feel every pain—physically, emotionally, spiritually, psychologically—that every human being has ever felt from when time began.

The cross allowed Jesus to feel every heartache ever borne by a child, every widow's pain as she takes a last glimpse of her husband and walks away from the sound of the casket closing, every wound that a boy feels when he loses a beloved parent, or every hurt that a girl feels when she is betrayed by a step-brother or an uncle or a friend of her father's. Every pain that has ever been felt, Jesus said, "I want to feel it."

I have been asked so many times, "What does it mean when Jesus said, 'It is finished'?" At that point, the whole act of redemption wasn't yet finished. Jesus had yet to take the blood to Heaven and sprinkle it on the Mercy Seat. He had yet to resurrect from the dead. What exactly was finished when Jesus uttered the words, "It is finished"?

What was finished was the moment that He had fully felt every pain every person has ever felt. He had felt the total sum package of every hurt.

When an agonizing person says, "God, why do You let these things happen?" or "God, where are You when I hurt so much?" or "God, where are You? I have nobody," Jesus says, "I know how you feel," because He does.

In my 30 years in the ministry, I have had thousands of counseling sessions in my office. Very rarely have I ever been able to say, "I understand." However, every time I have truthfully been able to say, "He understands." The songwriter says,

> "There's not a friend like the lowly Jesus,
> No, not one! No, not one!
> None else can heal all our soul's diseases,
> No, not one! No, not one!
>
> Jesus knows all about our struggles
> He will guide till the day is done;
> There's not a friend like the lowly Jesus,
> No, not one! No, not one!"

He does! Jesus says, "I see that 'emotional hand' on that hot exhaust. May I please remove it for you? May I pour on it the balm of Gilead—the ointment of gladness and joy? Would you consider that I understand the pain you have suffered because My hand has also felt the smokestacks of life? I have been injured. I can help give you the victory."

Our Saviour, Who is nothing less than the Son of the Living God, died on the cross for every man's sins. His wasn't just an act of mercy; it was an act of incredible friendship—an act of unbelievable love! He would like to be the Lover of your soul. He alone can start that healing process in a hurting heart.

CHAPTER FOUR

Perfect Peace
for Panicked People

Prerequisite Reading
Isaiah 26:1-9

W e live in a very complicated and complex society in this day and age. In the past couple years, I have noticed a measurable increase in the number of people experiencing extreme anxiety disorders or panic disorders. "The word anxiety comes from a Latin word meaning 'worried about the unknown,' and is also related to a Greek word meaning 'compress or strangle.' Are you being strangled by anxiety?"[1]

The *Diagnostic and Statistical Manual of Mental Disorders, Fourth Edition, Text Revision (DSM-IV-TR)* lists the following criteria for a panic attack:

A discrete period of intense fear of discomfort, in which four (or more) of the following symptoms developed abruptly and reached a peak within 10 minutes:

- palpitations, pounding heart, or accelerated heart rate
- sweating
- trembling or shaking

- sensations of shortness of breath or smothering
- feeling of choking
- chest pain or discomfort
- nausea or abdominal distress
- feeling dizzy, unsteady, lightheaded, or faint
- derealization (feelings of unreality) or depersonalization (being detached from oneself)
- fear of losing control or going crazy
- fear of dying
- paresthesias (numbness or tingling sensations)
- chills or hot flashes [2]

A panic attack is only one of several types of anxiety disorders according to the *DSM-IV-TR*. Agoraphobia, Obsessive-Compulsive Disorder (OCD), Posttraumatic Stress Disorder, Acute Stress Disorder, and phobias are all anxiety disorders which leave people emotionally weakened.

Even before September 11, 2001, about 19 million Americans suffered from anxiety and panic disorders, with one in ten having some degree of anxiety associated with mood swings, depression, fatigue, aches and pains, insomnia, and panic attacks. But after the horrendous terrorist acts that revised our basic world view, the umbrella of anxiety suddenly expanded to encompass the entire population, as Americans faced the shroud of insecurity and stress that came with a country under attack. Television screens were constantly filled with headlines denoting "anthrax anxiety" and "anxiety-ridden Americans under siege," and people began to worry about their ability to cope.

What felt like "going crazy" was really anxiety. And panic. And the endless gut-wrenching fear of the known and the unknown.[3]

Anxiety disorders are the most common of all emotional disorders, and according to the National Institute of Mental Health, the federal agency that conducts and supports research related to mental disorders, mental health, and the brain. In fact, these maladies are so widespread that mental health experts have named social anxiety the "Disorder of the Decade."[4]

I believe that these anxiety disorders are the by-product of the hyper-stressed lives we live. Technology was supposed to make our lives easier. Instead, an entirely new variety of problems has been introduced into our lives, and now we have new quandaries such as too many choices. When a person has limited choices, his life is simpler and he tends to be able to handle the situation. However, when a person moves faster, all of his senses have to be quickened at a higher rate. It's much easier to walk than it is to ride down the freeway.

After all, when have you ever heard of "walker's rage"? If someone cuts in front of you while walking and if you happen to bump into the person because he didn't use his "turn signal," generally, it's not a $1,200 damage issue. Lawyers seldom need to be called when two people happen to bump or even collide while walking on sidewalks. On the other hand, road rage has become a commonly used descriptive term, and sometimes the coroner's vehicle needs to be called in incidences of road rage.

When I was a boy, I remember watching Walter Cronkite discussing what he thought the twenty-first century would bring. Life would gently move along because robots and machines called computers would free up time with push-button ease. He really believed life would be incredibly easy.

If you own a computer, then you have probably "lost your salvation" on many occasions. I am just not sure that my computer has made my life any easier. I am always hearing statements like, "You need a software upgrade, Pastor Schaap" or "My computer just crashed with all of my work, Pastor Schaap!" On occasion, I would like to crash a few computers myself! I would like to drop them out of a third-floor window and let them crash on the ground beneath!

We move lightning fast. Complicated living is talking on your cell phone while manipulating your CD player and receiving a text message while you are weaving in and out of traffic on one of the busiest highways in any major city in America. Somehow, accomplishing all of that requires a different level of living than when Grandpa was hanging onto the reins of a workhorse pulling a farm wagon. What a different pace! Some of the complications we are discovering in our emotional levels and emotional problems which bleed over into relationship problems are no doubt a result of modern technology.

Modern living has opened the door to what I call "technology sins," which can quickly overwhelm our defenses. I believe we are becoming a frightened society unable to cope with the "monsters" we have created. I am reminded of Mary Shelley's famous horror novel, *Frankenstein*. The intention of Count Frankenstein in creating his monster from parts of dead bodies was for a life of service. In the beginning the monster was gentle and benign. But when people scorned it because of its ugliness, it became hateful and turned to murder—eventually even murdering his creator. The doctor's plan went dramatically awry, and instead of a servant, he created a terrorized and terrorizing individual.

Our modern technology allows us to bypass our moral barriers so quickly that children and teenagers can be bombarded with sin at a magnitude that 50 years ago could not have been comprehended. My grandfather would not be able to conceive what the Internet is capable of doing. We have finally reached the point where technology far surpasses our morality. Therefore, we are bombarded with intense pressures—the pressure of inconceivable temptation and the pressure of a fast pace—to name two of them!

We have reached a point where our senses are so exposed to

a world for which we were not designed or created, that we are unable to sustain our defenses, and we break down. With each repetitive round of temptation, and not just sinful temptation, comes the intrusion of busyness. Many people have forgotten that every gadget that seemingly makes life easier has an "off" button. Certainly, it is not immoral to turn off any of those gadgets including cell phones. Who says we have to live every minute of life being interrupted by phone calls? As technology and the pace of society has increased, panic and anxiety disorders have kept pace.

Our nation has also been devastated by several decades of divorced and single parents and eroding family values. Teens are much more unkind to their peers. Parents get out of synchronization with their children because they feel as though life is a stress-filled crucible in which they are held prisoner. "Dealing with stress makes us stronger; we can use it to amp us up to perform better, soar to greater heights. But dealing with anxiety, on the other hand, just makes us feel crazy."[5] The following are examples of adulthood stresses that must be taken in stride. If not dealt with properly, these kinds of stresses can lead to panic attacks and anxiety disorders:

- Financial setbacks
- A move
- A change in your primary love relationship
- Acquiring a new supervisor or new duties at work
- A recent incident that you found terribly humiliating
- A separation from a loved one—even when it's for a positive reasons such as marriage or college or a job promotion
- Having a child leave for kindergarten or college or reaching some other milestone that is meaningful to you
- A child having difficulties in school

- The death or loss of anyone in your circle of acquaintances, friends, or family
- A realization of your poor parenting style
- Hearing of someone's serious illness—even if the sufferer isn't someone central in your own life

Too Much Stress Can Cause:

Physical Problems

- Tiredness during the day
- Difficulty going to sleep
- Frequent waking at night
- Aches and pains
- Increased number of infections
- Palpitations
- High blood pressure
- Heart attacks
- Stroke
- Diarrhea
- Constipation
- Irritable bowel syndrome
- Stomach cramps
- Stomach ulcers
- Dental problems
- Mouth ulcers
- Skin problems
- Menstrual problems
- Hormonal imbalances

Psychological Problems

- Lack of interest in the world
- Vivid dreams
- Lack of motivation
- Listlessness
- Irritability
- Tearfulness
- Anxiety
- Poor performance at school
- Poor performance at work
- Eating problems
- Poor self-image
- Lack of patience
- Depression

Social Problems

- Increasing arguments at home
- Tendency to avoid people
- Abuse of alcohol, cigarettes, drugs
- Increased aggression
- Inappropriate behavior
- Overreaction to problems
- Ignoring problems[7]

- A parent's failing health
- Strong feelings of regret or sadness in your life, even if you aren't sure what initiated them
- Something that occurred in the present that led you to think about past difficulties
- Too much to do and not enough time for all of it
- An illness that sapped your strength and energy.[6]

Our lives have been invaded and robbed of the perfect peace that Isaiah prophesied in Isaiah 26:3, *"Thou wilt keep him in perfect peace, whose mind is stayed on thee: because he trusteth in thee."* This verse was engraved on a ceramic plaque that hung at the foot of my bed. My parents put it there when I was a junior-aged boy, and I read it every night before I went to bed. How I would love to give the gift of perfect peace to every person dealing with hurts.

- If I could, I would give a gift of perfect peace to those whose lives have been ravished by sin's predators at an early age.
- I would love to give a gift of perfect peace to those whose marriages are in trouble.
- I would love to give a gift of perfect peace to those whose homes are turned upside down by strife and contention.
- I would love to give a gift of perfect peace to those bus kids whose parents see the bus ministry as free babysitting.
- I would love to give a gift of perfect peace to those who must attend a public school and face incredible pressures from insecure peers trying to make a totally unnecessary statement of identity.
- I would love to give a gift of perfect peace to those who feel threatened because of the environments in which they live or work or go to school.
- I would love to give a gift of perfect peace to those who feel the pressure of financial collapse.

Stress Scores of Life Events (How stress affects you)

Death of spouse	100	Son or daughter leaving home	29
Divorce	73	Trouble with in-laws	29
Separation	65	Outstanding personal achievement	28
Jail term	63		
Death of close family member	63	Spouse begins or stops working	26
Personal injury or illness	53	Beginning or end of school or college	26
Marriage	50	Change in living conditions	25
Fired from work	47	Change in personal habits	24
Expelled from school	47	Trouble with boss	23
Marital reconciliation	45	Change in work hours or conditions	20
Retirement	45	Change in residence	20
Change in health of family member	44	Change in school or college	20
Pregnancy	40	Change in recreation	19
Sexual difficulties	39	Change in church activities	19
Gain of a new family member	39	Change in social activities	18
Business readjustment	38	A moderate loan or mortgage	17
Change in financial state	38	Change in sleeping habits	16
Death of a close friend	37	Change in number of family get-togethers	15
Change to different line of work	36	Change in eating habits	15
Change in number of arguments with spouse	35	Vacation	13
A large mortgage or loan	30	Christmas	12
Foreclosure of mortgage or loan	30	Minor violation of the law	11
Change in responsibilities at work	29		

The impact of several big changes in your life can build up over a period of time to cause too much stress. The aim of the life events table is to give you an idea of the amount of "life stress" you are experiencing at the present time. Add up the values of any events that have occurred in your life over the last year. If your score is over 250 and you have normal stress tolerance levels, then you may well be experiencing the symptoms associated with too much stress. If you have a low stress tolerance level, then a score of 150 may mean you have experienced enough stress to make you sick.[8]

- I would love to give a gift of perfect peace to those who have the pressure of making long commutes between home and work on a daily basis.

- I would love to give a gift of perfect peace to those college students who face incredible pressures of going to classes in the morning, working in the afternoon and evening, and trying to find some time to study.

I would give to every person I could the gift of perfect peace because I cannot think of anything more necessary in the world today than perfect peace.

- If I could, I would give perfect peace to the Middle East.
- If I could, I would give perfect peace to war-torn and strife-torn Iraq.
- If I could, I would give perfect peace to the people of Afghanistan.
- If I could, I would give perfect peace to the people in the Philippines where the Taliban is fighting.
- If I could, I would give perfect peace to any people in the world where leaders are posturing with angry words, vehement hatred, and making plans to terrorize other people.

An outer world without peace and an inner world lacking peace manifests itself in many ways. Damage is often inflicted beyond physical and emotional scars.

"Violence—experiencing it and witnessing it—is a huge issue in children's ability to learn," explains Dr. Jenny Horsman, author of *Too Scared to Learn*, who says she has interviewed hundreds of individuals whose learning has been affected by violence. "Anxiety really can close the senses down. I've had people who said they couldn't hear or see clearly in class, that the teacher's voice became a blur. It's as if their anxiety put them in a cocoon."[9]

If I could, I would give to everyone perfect peace because God said it is available to every person. The lack of peace we feel because of the pressures of life sometimes escalates into panic attacks and anxiety disorders. Many good Christian people struggle terribly with panic, and I want to encourage you.

1. You are not alone. If you suffer with these incredible panic attacks, realize that they touch the lives of pastors, youth directors, evangelists, Christian school teachers, deacons, and church people. None of God's people are immune to these very real times of upset. They touch people from all walks of life.

The American Psychiatric Association reports that more than 19 million Americans experience anxiety-disorder symptoms. These include overwhelming feelings of panic and fear, uncontrollable obsessive thoughts, intrusive memories, recurring nightmares, and physical reactions (nausea, migraines, muscle tension, sweating, among others).[10]

One great problem that these emotional distresses bring is the feeling of isolation and the mistaken belief that you are the only one being troubled. You feel so alone and isolated.

Thankfully, the majority of people have a panic attack only one time in their lives.

Research indicates that panic disorder usually begins between the ages of eighteen and thirty-five with a peak time of onset in the mid-twenties. And women are two to three times more likely than men to develop panic. Some experts believe that the number of men who suffer from panic has been underestimated because men are reluctant to admit difficulties with panic.[11]

About 25% of the people who have these attacks, have them repetitively and frequently, and the attacks are totally debilitating. That, in and of itself, often takes the person to a panic state worrying about when the next panic attack will happen.

2. Don't fall for the lie that you are an exception. The Devil wants you to believe that your case is different from all other scenarios. He also wants you to believe that you will never overcome this problem. Contrary to what the Devil would have you believe, the case studies all read alike. The following is an example of one study I read, and almost anyone's name could be inserted as being the person who reported these characteristics:

Jane S. is 22 years old. She was spending the weekend in a small midwestern town with her aunt and uncle, which she frequently did. She enjoyed walking in the early morning, and one day she decided to venture out alone for a 2-mile walk in an area she knew well. Nearly at the turnaround point, as she crossed over a small bridge, she felt a sudden wave of terror come over her for no apparent reason. Her knees felt rubbery, she felt dizzy and sweaty, and her heart was pounding. It was a terrifying experience. She knew that she had to return to the house as quickly as possible. That was Jane's first panic attack.[12]

I have had pastors call and say, "Brother Schaap, I was in the pulpit the other day, and without any warning, I just felt such an impending feeling of dread and doom. I felt like I was just going to go crazy." Another said, "I just wanted to curse and say, 'Forget it all! I'm leaving! I have tendered my resignation! It's all over for me!' "

I assured these good men that everyone is confronted by a panic attack at one time or another. Many a parent comes to me when their children are anywhere between 3 and 40 and says, "You won't believe what it is like rearing kids!"

Those of us who have children have all had episodes during which we did not think we would be able to keep our sanity. Feelings of impending doom invaded our minds. Feelings of desperately needing to escape come. You want to get in a car, drive as far as you can until you run out of gasoline, then get out of the car, run until you exhaust yourself, and fall into a ditch to die. These kinds of emotional pressures touch the lives of many people.

Don't fall for the Devil's lie that you are an exception and cannot possibly win this battle. Don't maximize your problem unnecessarily! We are all built of the same kind of chemistry, the same type of circuitry, the same type of blood vessels, and the same kind of heart which pumps blood through your body. We all face the same kind of pressures, the same Devil, the same world, the same lusts, the same flesh, the same enemies, and the same sins.

3. Don't expect a quick cure. One of the great problems in a society that is so technologically minded is that we erroneously think that our problems can be fixed as quickly as they began. We want to race down the "cure" path as fast as we drive a car down an expressway, and that will not happen! Time will be a great ally to you as you fix your problems. It takes time to rear a child and go through the stages of infant, toddler, adolescent, teenage years, etc.

When my daughter turned four and my son was about a year, I was advised by a very wise man to enjoy our children fully during what he called the "precious years": the ages between four and ten. He reminded me that when children reach about four years of age, they become excellent communicators, and they really warm to their parents. There is no competition with the opposite gender. They will curl up in your lap, show lots of affection, and ask spiritual questions. They believe Mom and Dad are just short of God! "Enjoy the precious years," he admonished me, "because after the age of ten, it changes."

He was so right! My wife and I faced changes at 10, at 11, at 15, at 16, at 17…! I am being slightly humorous because I never met an age with our children that I didn't fully enjoy. Every stage of life has its own different pressures, but you will get through everything. In fact, you will no doubt get all the way through life to the cemetery! You will get through every problem. There are no permanent problems. Even sin is not a permanent problem because there's forgiveness, grace, mercy, the power of the Holy Ghost, and the promises of God. In order to get through this time in your life, you must get away from this "cell-phone mentality" and this "DSL-speed mentality." You want to zoom at 100 miles per hour and fix every problem with the click of a mouse or double click your problems away. I sometimes wish it did, but it doesn't happen that way, and it will not happen with you or any of us. When problems come, let me suggest one reason why anxiety disorders and panic attacks come to people in our society. I believe it is God's way of telling us that we are going a little too fast. I believe they are God's way of slowing us down.

When God steps into your life, you really should listen. When a couple faces a marital crisis, suppose the husband wants to punch the accelerator, go faster, and say, "If she can't keep up with me, she can just go find someone else." God sends problems to a person to ask him to re-direct his attention to something else He wants the person to notice. God does not allow panic attacks and anxiety disorders and emotional pressures because He doesn't know what to do about them. He is trying to say, "I want you to redirect your attention elsewhere."

Allow me to share several statements of practical advice that will help you understand the following questions:

- Why do these types of emotional pressures come?
- Why do you face panic attacks and anxiety disorders?

1. **Too many loose ends.** Brother Hyles called these "unfinished starts." Eight hours after you started the washing machine, the wet laundry is still in the machine waiting to be placed in the dryer. The cross stitch you started for a wedding gift has not been completed, and the wedding has already passed. The booties you

started knitting for a baby are still sitting in the dusty knitting basket, and that baby is now 14 years old! These and other unfinished tasks remind you of all these things that you started but never finished.

Ideally, the number of starts in life should be equal to the same number of finishes in life. The Apostle Paul so wisely said, "*This one thing I do....*" (Philippians 3:13) The practical application of that Scripture passage is, "I'm doing **one** thing because I am going to finish that **one** thing I have started. Then I am going to do another **one** thing, and I am going to finish that **one** thing, and then go to another **one** thing." Paul did not want to bring confusion to his life by going in 50 different directions at one time.

When I became the pastor of First Baptist Church in 2001, I was barraged by good friends of Brother Hyles' and mine asking me to accept honorary degrees at their commencement exercises that year as a means of showing their encouragement and support. I categorically said "no" to all of these invitations because I knew that I did not need to take on multiple starts while I was starting something as huge as pastoring First Baptist Church. I was very flattered, honored, and appreciative, but I knew the truth of Philippians 3:13, "*...this one thing I do....*"

In the same way, when you start a marriage, you probably don't need to take on a ministry the very same day. That is why the Bible teaches that before a man goes off to war and leaves his wife, he should take a year to cheer up his wife. The Bible is teaching that he has started something huge and to make sure he has the wherewithal to sustain and finish the marriage before he takes on other major beginnings.

Unfinished items of business nag at your human circuitry. As a general rule, I don't think one big start caused the panic; I believe it is a series of unfinished beginnings. These seemingly insurmountable obstacles can be overcome.

Do not misunderstand me! There are some large issues in life that must be faced. Perhaps some predator took advantage of you as a child and violated you multiple times. Perhaps you never told your parents, or a counselor, or your pastor, or your spouse, and you have hidden that hurt deep within you. For that kind of monumental hurt, seek some counseling from a godly person. There is help for this horrific event.

The long-term consequences of childhood sexual assault (CSA) vary because the outcome is very much influenced by the child's perception of the abuse, the family, and its reaction when the abuse was disclosed. Extensive exploration in the 1980s and the 1990s indicates that there is, indeed, an association between CSA and wide range of problems in adulthood; for example: depression, suicidal behaviors, eating disorders, interpersonal difficulties, self-harm, anger management problems, and anxiety disorders."[13]

Perhaps you lost your father or your mother as a child. The remaining parent then rejected you because she was losing her husband, and she couldn't be both a dad and a mom to you. Maybe a relative took you in, and as payment, you were repeatedly violated, and you lost your purity. Those are big issues that need the help of a godly counselor.

In my experience, I find that the majority of people, who go through some very difficult anxiety problems, are people who have many starts with very few or no finishes. When you don't finish them and bring them to a conclusion, it results in incredible pressure on you.

2. A cluttered life. Disorganized living leads to discouragement which leads to depression. I love cleanliness. To me, clean is an attitude. I think having an attitude of cleanliness is a part of my Dutch heritage. The bottom line is that I love clean!

I can handle some clutter, but only for a little while. Every morning, the reset button is pushed in my church office.

Everything is cleared off my desk except the material I am going to handle that day.

At Pastors' School time, I get so busy that my assistant and I sometimes leave the desk piled high with mail and emergency messages and appointment reminders, etc. Clutter weighs heavily

---

Some bites of advice from the postscript, "100 Bites of Advice for the Rushed, Impatient, Harried, and Distractible":

1. Never give up.

2. Have as many handles on happiness as you can.

3. If in doubt about how to interpret a situation, let it be positive.

4. Do random acts of kindness.

5. Build character by doing one thing each day that is difficult but good for you to do.

6. Give out compliments liberally.

7. When you say hello to someone, smile.

8. Clean up your diet.

9. Get a "clutter buddy" if you need one.

10. Listen to doctors carefully, but don't worship them. Even God gives us free choice.

11. Spend 15 to 30 minutes each day confronting your clutter.

12. Start a vigorous, regular exercise program.

13. Break down tasks and projects into smaller steps.

14. Free yourself of clutter by donating or throwing out belongings.

15. Practice "OHIO." Only handle mail or papers one time.

16. Make frequent use of lists.

17. Use color coding to help you organize.

18. Use a bulletin board to organize your tasks and projects.

19. Use more than one alarm clock to get up on time.

20. Plan your day the night before.

21. Use timers to keep you on tract.

22. Have a daily quiet time to do your paperwork.

23. Give rewards for a job well done.

24. Keep the desk clear if you can.

25. Simplify your life.

26. Establish a rule of no arguments at the dinner table.

27. Classical music is healing.

28. Keep a journal.

29. Finish one project before starting another.

30. A phrase that is comforting to many: *"Be still, and know that I am God."* (Psalm 46)[14]

on my mind to the point where I find myself looking into the office and thinking, "I don't even want to go in there." I probably spend 10 to 15 percent of my life organizing the remaining 85 to 90 percent! I spend a good deal of my time organizing my life because I cannot stand the clutter of life. I also keep my car immaculate because a disorderly car clutters my mind like a cluttered office bothers me. The clutter of life wears down those who live disorganized, unfinished lives. Take time to be organized! You are using a lot of mental energy to remember things you do not need to remember if you were only organized.

Let me put it in computer lingo. If you fill an 80-gigabyte hard drive with 79-gigabytes of information, so much is stored in the computer that it takes a long time to sort through all the clutter of unneeded files to find the one you need. When you start computer jobs and finish them, download them to storage disks and file them to eliminate clutter. Don't keep them on the computer for the next few years! Your computer will not run efficiently.

The human mind works much the same way as a computer. I know that I do not possess a mind capable of remembering all that I need to remember and then also take care of others' problems. My mind is very simple compared to most people's. I do not mean that I am a simple person. Why overload the brain and waste energy trying to remember some facts that could easily be written on an 8fi x 11 sheet of paper and filed?

Disorganized surroundings are an automatic indicator of a person who is a candidate for a panic attack or an anxiety disorder. The endless clutter says that you do not know what to do with the "ends" of your life. As a result, laundry is piled high in the laundry area. Dirty dishes overflow the sink and kitchen counters. Newspapers are scattered in several places. Learning how to organize your life and getting rid of unnecessary clutter is one way to help eliminate the onset of panic disorders. If unnecessary clutter describes your life, I would suggest looking in the

Yellow Pages for the word "dumpster," order one, and have a throwing-out party. Enact a new rule in your life: If you haven't used it in six months, get rid of it.

3. Marginal health. We live in a society of extremes. One extreme is represented by those who do not have a job and do not care about having a job because others' hard-earned tax money pays for them to live, and they enjoy sleeping more than eight hours a day. My advice is to get a life and stop mooching off of others.

The other extreme is represented by a family where the husband works full-time, the wife works part-time or even full-time, and in order to have any kind of family life with children, you fall into bed by 11:30 at night and get up at 5:00 a.m. to begin anew. Maybe a man can handle this kind of schedule, but a woman cannot!

Women who take on extra jobs or work outside of the home and have more than one child at home should be getting at least eight hours of sleep every night. It wouldn't be bad for her to take a nap in the afternoon on top of that. Proper rest is very important, and if you are not getting a appropriate amount of rest, you are living a life of marginal health.

4. Eating carelessly. If your idea of a balanced diet is a KitKat candy bar with an ice cream cone followed by a can of Coca-Cola, please don't come to see me when you suffer with panic attacks. I will tell you that you must learn to eat some decent foods. One rule of thumb is if it is green, it's probably good for you.

When people come to see me about panic attacks, I always say, "Tell me your diet."

Often I am asked, "What does that have to do with emotional problems?"

My usual response to that question is "What does breathing have to do with living?"

When you don't eat a balanced diet, more than likely your disposition will change. You start snapping at people and getting temperamental.

Have you ever taken the time to realize that food damned your soul? Eve ate a fruit from a tree—something that looked good, smelled good, and tasted good to her. God is trying to teach us that what we eat has a direct bearing upon our spirit—how we think and how we feel. Having marginal health because of poor eating habits will cause a condition where we are highly susceptible to anxiety problems, emotional disorders, and panic attacks.

Dieting should not always be a way of life. Rather, you need to learn to live a lifestyle of proper eating and exercise. If you absolutely cannot drop the five or ten pounds you wish to lose, stop criticizing the way you are.

Panic attacks come when a person consistently lives on his reserve.

5. Maximum expectations and minimal planning. For instance, the pastor preaches about reaching the world, you surrender to the mission field, and you have zero planning. What plans do you have for following through with your decision? In some ways, I would almost rather have a person not make the decision because that decision can complicate the emotions. Especially is this true if he goes back to his former lifestyle with the change in his heart but without the proper planning in his life. The person will frustrate himself. He is open to the Devil's lie of being the kind of the person who cannot measure up. The spiritual decision actually defeats him before he starts! A plan should be set in place to follow through.

A classic example of this point is a couple planning marriage with zero money, high debt, and no game plan. They have yet to finish anything they have started in life; quitting jobs is a frequent scenario in their lives. This engaged couple came to see me and asked, "How soon do you think we can get married, Pastor?" This couple should get married only when they firm up their prenuptial agreement with the divorce lawyer because that's exactly where that relationship will soon be! They will wallow in a marriage they should not enter at this time in their lives. Some Christians who marry prematurely are just good enough Christians not to get divorced. Their marriage will become a seesaw relationship that will flounder like a boat carrying too much weight and not enough horsepower to propel it. Couples should work to get their planning right so their expectations and planning meet each other.

Perhaps you have great dreams for starting a business. Without a game plan, those dreams cause frustration, and oftentimes you face indebtedness and have nothing to show for the expenditure and work. You must have a plan in place for every dream; otherwise, the dream is nothing but a fantasy that quickly turns into a nightmare.

6. An imbalanced schedule. Scheduled people tend to be much more secure and relaxed. For instance, go to bed and get up at roughly the same time every day. You should be in bed within 15 to 30 minutes of your set time each night and get up within a few minutes of your set time each morning. Don't schedule your life down to having only five minutes of leeway; rather, schedule it within zones. Eat at generally the same time every day. Get into a rhythm and a cadence of life, and that rhythm and cadence will sustain you through the emotional upheavals of life.

7. An absence of affection and romance. If you are married and your spouse has panic problems, ask yourself how affectionate you are toward your spouse. If your husband is prone to emotional roller-coasters, as your counselor, I would automatically ask, "What is your love life like toward your husband?" People who receive affection from a spouse find a tremendous emotional security. Rarely have I ever talked to anyone who has an emotional problem way-out-of-kilter consistently, who comes from a very affectionate marriage.

A missionary friend of mine in Romania visited an orphanage

where he saw hundreds of babies lying listlessly in cribs doing nothing—not even crying. He asked a nurse, "What's wrong with these babies?"

"They're dying," she said.

"They don't look sick," he said. "From what disease?"

"The disease," the nurse said, "is the absence of a mother's touch and love."

"I don't understand. If they are dying, are you sure they don't have some communicable disease or some sort of impairment like a heart defect?"

"No," she shook her head sadly. "A child that is not touched dies."

A mother with a baby should stroke that baby, touch that baby lovingly, rub that baby with lotion, and let that baby feel the touch of her hand and the cooing sound of her voice. Touch provides an incredible security for a baby. Those children who do not receive that kind of affection deal with many emotional problems later on in life.

Husbands and wives need to share the kind of physical touch that doesn't always lead to the intimate marital relationship. Use the kindness of a touch, the gentleness of a caress, the warmhearted stroking that says, "I value you as a person." People who have that acceptance are much more emotionally stable than people who do not. Even though they may think they have a hot romantic life, it is not hot romance that often is lacking. The sweet, friendly, kind, companionable caressing and affection are often what is missing in a marriage.

How to Cope With Panic

1. **Live in the Scriptures.** When an emotional crisis comes, that is not a time to simply say, "I have my prayer time." You need to quadruple the amount of time you spend in the Scriptures. When you experience an emotional time of imbalance, that is not

a time to race through the Bible to see how many chapters you can read. Slow down your Bible reading, put it in first gear, and just very slowly read the words. The Words of God will prove to be invaluable to you during these times.

I have actually had people say to me, "Pastor, I have this emotional problem, and I read 125 chapters yesterday. It didn't help!"

It's not volume! It's absorption! Let the Word of Christ dwell in you richly. Start and end each day with the Bible. Let me make a suggestion. Before you go to bed, open your Bible to Psalm 119 which is what I call a medically healing chapter. This Bible chapter about the Bible itself is divided into 22 sections. Take eight to ten minutes to read and savor just one of those eight-verse sections just before you turn off the light and go to sleep. Think about what you read as you drift off to sleep because one of the great problems of emotional imbalance is sleep disruption. I promise you that reading the Bible will help you sleep a little better. It is far better than a sleeping pill or a sleeping aid.

2. Memorize Scripture. I am not suggesting that you memorize huge portions of Scripture. You already have enough on your mind. Rather, memorize verses that relate to your problem and affliction. Write them on a 3x5 card, and "chew" on them all day long. Ponder on a phrase, or a couple of words, or a thought throughout the day.

3. Do a Bible study on fear and on faith. All emotional problems are an attack against faith by using fear. Fear is the number-one killer of stable Christians.

4. Visit nursing homes and hospitals. Spend as much time as possible encouraging other people who have obvious, legitimate concerns. When you go through these emotional problems, you become very self-centered, and you turn all of the focus on yourself. One of the most dangerous things you can do is start looking at what's wrong with you because you will find out that everything is. You will discover that you are unfaithful and inconsistent, and you will think every kind of impossible thought. You will even think of suicide or murder! You will eventually believe that you are nothing but a despicable, worthless person, and you will denigrate yourself to the point of total uselessness. Then you could say, "I should just end it all!" Emotional problems force you into dangerous periods of introspection.

Don't look at yourself; visit a nursing home. When you leave, a most glorious feeling should come over you: YOU can walk out of there. When you visit those good people and take a carnation or a Gospel tract or a piece of sugar-free candy or a piece of fruit to them, sit down and say, "Tell me about your day." Brighten the corner of another human being's dull, drab, and unattractive life from which most can never leave. Their next stop is the cemetery. As you start giving people an uplifting message, you will get your mind off of yourself. You will also be your own greatest medicine—the best antidepressant you have ever used in your life.

> Helping someone else is the secret to happiness.
> –Booker T. Washington

"Bake some chocolate chip cookies for a widow lady," Brother Hyles used to say, "and take them to her, sit down for a half an hour or an hour, and ask her to show you pictures of her husband and her children. Cheer her by your concern for her life. I promise you will leave there saying, 'I feel so much better!' " When you take the focus off of yourself, you will soon free yourself of depression and panic. His perfect peace that is promised in Isaiah 26:3 will return to your life.

CHAPTER FIVE

Bringing Order to My Disordered World

Prerequisite Reading
Isaiah 26:3-9

I have a tremendous respect for those sincere professionals who do their best to try to help people who struggle with emotional and mental difficulties. I am more of a practical advisor, and I am not a qualified professional in the area of psychiatry or psychology. Personally, I do not mind psychology which is the study of the soul, *pseucos lagos*. As a preacher and pastor, I do believe I am very qualified to study the soul, as any theologian or student of the Bible would be qualified. In both I Thessalonians and Ephesians, the Apostle Paul addressed the subject of completeness—the whole man. Colossians 2:10 says, *"And ye are complete in him...."* In order to serve Him to our greatest ability, we need to be fully functioning spiritually, physically, and emotionally.

This chapter will address more of the reasons why people are subject to anxiety disorders and panic attacks. These issues

> Our anxiety does not empty tomorrow of its sorrow, but only empties today of its strength.
> –Charles Spurgeon

are becoming more and more pronounced as stable people from good, solid homes have their lives turned upside down by these anxious moments. They feel the whole world seems to be closing in on them and attacking them with a vengeance. The physical symptoms feel like the onset of a heart attack or a stroke. The condition sometimes becomes so explosive and so frequent that the person becomes reclusive.

I do not pretend that I have all the answers to cure or help prevent these times of anxiety. Allow me to share some common-sense thinking that will perhaps help those who suffer with panic. In my research from reading books and articles authored by both psychiatrists and psychologists and from talking to many doctors in person, basically only two treatments exist for this in the medical world: drugs and a behavioral thinking change. Professionals strive to teach people to think differently about these situations.

Anxiety is a normal part of life; physical sensations of one sort or another are a normal part of life, and it's impossible to eliminate either. The event that absolutely must be eliminated to eliminate panic is catastrophic thinking—the "what-if" thinking, the "I'm-in-danger" interpretation. The normal physical sensations and normal worrisome thoughts remain just that—normal and manageable. How do you do that? You learn to apply three steps: Stop-Refocus-Breathe—The SRB Method.

1. Stop. The very instant you experience the slightest hint of discomfort, the first whisper that something feels amiss or different in your body, immediately say: STOP IT!

2. Refocus. Focus furiously on anything present-centered. Use your senses to focus concretely on what you can see, hear, smell, touch or taste in your immediate environment. Try to identify all the sounds, even the faintest of them.

3. Breathe. Begin controlled breathing that will further occupy your concentration and prevent your mind from having the chance to sneak back to the "what ifs."

To the extent you perform these three steps, your anxiety will diminish.[1]

The SRB method is using the tool of behavioral thinking. I specialize in behavioral thinking, too; it is called preaching. My parents called a change in behavioral thinking an attitude adjustment. (They also called an attitude adjustment a spanking!) Many good Christian people struggle terribly with anxiety and panic, and I want to address areas that exacerbate these attacks.

1. Posttrauma Depression. Very simply, *post* means "after" and *trauma* means "any event that has traumatized or distressed your life emotionally or physically."

Community-based studies reveal a lifetime prevalence for Posttraumatic Stress Disorder of approximately 8% of the adult population in the United States. Studies of at-risk people (i.e., groups exposed to specific traumatic incidents) yield variable findings, with the highest rates (ranging between one-third and more than half of those exposed) found among survivors of rape, military combat and captivity; and ethnically or politically motivated internment and genocide.[2]

Undergoing major cancer therapy or major surgery, recovering from a marital setback, losing a spouse in death or divorce, losing a parent or miscarrying a baby are all examples of traumatic experiences that emotionally drain a person.

PTSD, also once known as shell shock or battle fatigue, affects hundreds of thousands of individuals who have survived the trauma of natural disasters such as earthquakes, accident disasters such as airplane crashes, war, school shootings, crimes, and effects of abuse or neglect as children or adults. Although its symptoms can occur soon after the event, PTSD often surfaces several months or even years later. Symptoms include repeated episodes of re-experiencing the traumatic event that can happen in sudden, vivid memories accompanied by very painful emotions that seem to have no cause. Panic attack and anxiety often result from PTSD experiences.[3]

Some events are not necessarily bad in and of themselves, but the events can still be very traumatic. You walk away from the casket at the cemetery and then try to get your life back in order. However, you have suffered an enormous emotional drain, and it will take some time to refill the reserve. When you try to feel normal again too quickly before you have replenished that emotional reserve, it is like living on the edge with poor health. Living on the edge causes panic attacks and anxiety. Pushing your health right to the limit, living on minimal amounts of sleep, eating very poorly, or facing financial crises every time a bill is due, cause incredible pressures. The drain is so phenomenal, that if you're not careful, you will overextend yourself. These traumatic upsets to your already-depleted resources can bring on an anxiousness that can push you over your limit to the point where you become anti-social and withdrawn. Some even pull away from God.

Many people come to my office for counseling and say, "Pastor, I have been diagnosed by my doctor or my psychologist as having panic attacks or with adult attention deficit disorder or as bipolar."

I ask the person, "How is your quiet time with the Lord?" or "How is your walk with God?" or "What is your meditation time like?" They are generally embarrassed as they admit it is non-existent. They are not attempting to replenish themselves with what they desperately need to help them through the trauma they have experienced.

Addressing this problem of PTSD reminds me of finances. One author's philosophy of money is to have more than one source of income because of so many drains on the finances. Sometimes the problem of more out-go than income has to be faced and fixed. Some people are deeply in debt. Let me further explain. A good couple in our church bought a new house and a new vehicle because they had a great job and could easily make the payments. Everything about their future looked secure until they suffered an unexpected, major setback; and as a result, they had to downsize their house; they lost their new vehicle; and their credit was damaged. This couple came to see me because the wife was suffering from incredible anxiousness and was emotionally on edge. Thankfully, in that case, the husband was holding her hand through this crisis time.

Posttrauma depression is the result of not enough emotional income to balance the outgo. When a major hit comes such as a death, a miscarriage, or even a new birth, depression seeps in. Sometimes within three months of a wedding or the birth of a baby, depression strikes with a ferocity. Both of these are positive events, but they still place a tremendous drain on people. Generally, the person doesn't take the time to recover sufficiently after giving out a maximum output for these special times of life.

When I became the pastor of First Baptist Church of Hammond, I decided to have a spring break following Pastors' School. So many people give out at a maximum output during this conference. Believe it or not, some people literally put in 140-plus hours a week during Pastors' School. For me, I need a couple of good solid weeks to get over Pastors' School—with one day of almost nothing but constant sleep. A conference like Pastors' School causes a tremendous drain of emotional resources because for many, it can be nothing but a constant outgo!

I found it interesting to note that one of the most famous evangelists in America's history who preached city-wide crusades wrote that every night after he preached just one 30-minute sermon, he slept 14 hours. Some would have accused this man of being lazy. The one who would make such an accusation couldn't be further from the truth! This evangelist built a huge ministry, and multitudes were saved through his ministry. He was not a lazy man; people have a difficult time understanding the emotional drain others feel.

That emotional drain must be refilled, and if it's not refilled, you might well be a candidate for panic attacks. You are living in a zone where you are in danger of going over the edge if some traumatic event were to enter your life.

Living a sinful life and behaving in a way that you know is inconsistent with your Christian life brings guilt and remorse. "Guilt is one of the most isolating and paralyzing of all emotions, and depression and guilt often travel hand in hand."[4] Both are powerful anxiety builders. When your conscience is guilty and you are trying to put up a good front, you feel an enormous emotional drain. "Two feelings in particular can follow traumatic events and feel overwhelming—self-hatred and shame."[5] That is one reason why healthy Christians live righteous lives—not because they always enjoy living righteously more, but because they welcome the freedom and the healthier feeling and emotional buoyancy they have in not sinning.

2. Resisting the natural ebbs and flows of life. Obviously, every day cannot be sunny, and every day cannot be an upbeat, positive day. Certainly a person chooses to be a positive person with a happy outlook; but gray days, blustery days, stormy days, and rainy days—physically and emotionally—will come into life.

Some days a couple's marriage will not mesh well. Days will come when you look at your spouse and at yourself and say, "What in the world is wrong with us?" Write off those days by saying, "I'm in one of those ebb days! Things aren't flowing quite right at the moment!"

My wife and I both love the ocean. At sunrise we love to just sit and watch the waves gently come in. Anyone who watches the water carefully will notice it has an ebb and a flow. Just like the ocean waters break on a beach, there is a constant ebb and flow of life; the emotions are high, and the emotions are low—mountain peaks and valleys come into life. Some people need to come to the realization that they cannot have a great day every day. You **can** choose to have a great attitude or a great disposition every day! You **can** talk to a great God every day, and you **can** do a great deed for someone every day, but you cannot have a great day every day.

Years ago, my grandparents often spent a good deal of time in Florida where they had a summer home. Grandpa had something that I really loved—a boat! My family would vacation there for a week to spend time with them. I loved going out on the Atlantic Ocean with Grandpa. Just he and I would go out for several miles to go deep-sea fishing.

I was only about six or seven years old, and Grandpa would say, "Why don't you drive the boat?" Grandpa's boat was only a 19-foot boat with a 33-horsepower engine. His suggestion was dangerous, but I knew I was safe with Grandpa standing beside me. Driving that boat through the channel, with huge ocean liners coming and going and speed boats zipping through about 60 miles per hour as well as the tremendous currents, made the maneuvering tricky. I would take the helm from Grandpa, and I would fight the big waves coming at us. I wanted to make that boat go a certain direction. Soon I began shaking from the seeming impossible task I was performing as a little boy.

Grandpa would calmly say, "Son, don't fight the ocean. Work with it! Pick a spot about a mile ahead of you where you generally want to go, and let the waves pull you, and let the engine take you. Don't wrestle with the ocean—it's so much bigger than you are."

We human beings need to realize that life is so much bigger than we are. Just like I couldn't wrestle with the ocean, we cannot wrestle with life. Instead, we must let life come to us at the pace God decides to bring it to us. We may want to rush at it and try to elbow our way through life, but the correct way is to let it come to us.

Grade schooler, let junior high come to you. Junior higher, let high school come to you. High schooler, let college come to you. Young adult, let marriage come to you. Don't make the mistake of racing after life because you will soon find yourself fighting the waves of life—the ebbs and flows, if you please. Don't fight the so-called bad days; rather, go through them to the bright spot on the other side! Deal with what each today brings.

3. Holding to one stage of life too long. Too many parents hold onto a child's stage too long after the child has long since left that stage.

Let me testify. My wife, daughter, and granddaughter went out of town for two and a half days. I like to take advantage of a time like that to spend time with my son or my son-in-law. I already had been formulating some ideas of my own, but before I could broach the subject, my son came to me and said, "Dad, with Mom out of town for a little while, do you think we could take this time and spend some extra time together?"

Truthfully, his request meant a lot to me. My mind went back to when he was a junior-aged boy and would call me at work to ask, "Dad, when are you coming home? We'll play football in the living room!" I would go home, and I would get on my knees to play football with my son in the living room for an hour or two or three. Then we would go outside to play catch or basketball.

We did get together to do some "guy things," and we enjoyed the time together. When I went to bed that night, I was reflecting on the day, and I dreamed that he was a little boy again. I woke up about 2 o'clock in the morning with tears running down my cheeks from reliving those wonderful years when a junior-aged boy couldn't get enough of his daddy.

At this writing Ken is engaged to a very precious young lady, and on December 17, 2005, they will become husband and wife. Ken is trying to save money and prepare for a wedding, work as many hours as he can, and also finish college. I don't see him as much as I would like to see him. For just a little while after that time we had together, I was very tempted to wish I could go back to those days when he was a junior-aged boy.

Because I am a very sentimental person, I listened very carefully to Brother Hyles teaching how he had to guard his feelings. Now I guard my feelings as do those who protect Fort Knox because those feelings can so quickly get away from me. I can easily start feeling that I am way too busy and begin wondering, "Did I miss any special moments?" As I search my heart, I realize that I didn't waste any time, and I am so thankful that I did all I knew to do during those precious years.

Parents, let me warn you, if you are not willing to let your children proceed to the next stage, you are setting the stage for dealing with anxious disorders, emotional trauma, and panic attacks. Anxiety comes when a person will not proceed to the next stage of life. Even church families struggle with going to the next level. When I accepted the pastorate of First Baptist Church, some people had a difficult time letting go of Brother Hyles. I told the people to grieve for him until they died of old age. I myself missed him terribly, and I still do.

When I became the pastor, I kept a couple of pictures of him in the office, and I soon found that I could not deal with it. One of the custodians played his sermons while he was working, and for the first two or three years I was pastor, I had to shut the door or leave the office. Hearing his voice preaching would send me on the floor in waves of convulsive, violent crying. I realized that I could not effectively pastor the people if I could not stop sobbing because I was so sad that he was gone.

I took down all of the pictures and put them in a box until the time came when I could deal with seeing them. I decided not to listen to his sermons. I took everything out of the office that reminded me of him except for a chair and a clock that my wife and I bought for him. For some reason, those two items did not bother me, and if I had to explain why, I could not. I had to be very careful not to live in a zone that I could not deal with emotionally. I had to realize that I did not take Brother Hyles' place; I had to realize that I was taking the place that God had for me.

A mother's "little" boy got married seven years ago, and his room still looks exactly like it did when he was in high school. When she goes to visit that room, her husband knows it because his wife's eyes are puffy when he gets home from work. Change that room!

When Jaclynn went to her first day of school, I cried just like I knew I would. All too soon, she graduated from Hammond Baptist High School. She couldn't wait to go to the college dorms because she was a social butterfly, and she loved making friends. On her last night at home, she began to play the piano. I was already in bed, and as I listened to her play, the tears came. I knew that an era was over. When I walked her down the aisle to give her away, I was ready. I had a wonderful time at the wedding—until I went home. I walked by her piano, touched it, and my tears flowed just like a river. We also converted her bedroom into our laundry room the very next week.

Some people need to convert the shrines they have for their children into a laundry room, a billiards room, a board-game room, or a place to display their shotguns and knife collection! Sentiment and emotion is attached to many of the eras of life; and if you build shrines to your children, you take yourself into a zone that traumatizes your emotions. Don't hold tightly to a particular stage of life!

In my study of this topic, I discovered that a high percentage of people who struggle in this area are people who work with youth! Why? They face constant pressures to stay young, to keep up, and to be accepted; they give maximum output with under-compensation. Teenagers are not known to compensate well for the amount of effort another gives. There's a grasping for youth—a constant desire to maintain a youthful image and a youthful zeal.

4. A battle for control. The mind battles to regain the control it believes to be lost. James 1:8 says, *"A double minded man is unstable in all his ways."* I believe that a double-minded person is a controlling individual—a person who feels that someone or something has grabbed control of a certain area of his life. For instance, a mother "loses" control of her son to a daughter-in-law. Contrary to what she believes, that daughter-in-law is not taking her place! The daughter-in-law is merely taking HER place in the marriage.

We must learn to hold loosely to people and to the possessions of this world. Spiritually speaking, your children are not yours. You are a steward of **God's** children; they belong to Jesus Christ, and when you start possessing them as though you are their controller, you are setting the stage for an emotional disorder or panic attacks.

In the workplace, some people want to control their office environment and cannot allow anyone else to have any kind of authority. They feel threatened by any new employees. Some established people cannot stand new people coming into the work force because they automatically think that person is there to take their job. My advice is to just do your job! Nobody can replace anyone! Learn to put aside that selfish, insecure feeling that somehow you are losing your position or place. When a person is emotionally disturbed and distracted and extended way beyond his ability to control his life, often it is because he has been trying to control another's territory!

A father feels like he has lost control to a son-in-law. Personally, I believe I had the greatest father-in-law in the world. He was always available if we needed him, but he never pushed himself into our lives. He let us go through our ups and downs, and he allowed us struggle. Because of his example, I want to give the same deference to my son-in-law and future daughter-in-law. They will never have to worry about intrusions from their in-laws. I know what a great gift my father-in-law gave to me.

A youth director feels that he has lost control of the teens. A pastor gets older and feels he is losing control of a church. An employer gets older and feels as though he is losing control of his business. A time will surely come when every person has to let go of some control.

5. Strong-willed people who have not mastered the art of peaceful surrender. This type of person must always win. If you are the kind of person who is hyper-competitive, if you get angry about a board game, if you are someone who yells at coaches and umpires, you are a candidate for panic attacks and anxiety disorders.

On our one-year anniversary, my wife and I were in Estes Park, Colorado. I noticed a Monopoly game at the place where we were staying, so my wife and I decided to play a game. As the game progressed, my wife was beating me hands down because she happened to own Boardwalk and Park Place and a few others. All I owned were two worthless pieces of property that netted me a couple of dollars when she landed on them. Every time I landed on any of her properties, it seemed like I owed her $2,000! To top it off, she invariably landed on the FREE parking and claimed all the "free" money.

My fiercely competitive nature finally reached its boiling point, and I grabbed the game and threw it against the wall. Sanity overtook me, so I left the room, took a long walk, cooled down, and returned—a little sheepishly. It was a good day for me when I became a grown-up enough person to lose graciously.

If you have a competitive spirit, learn the art of letting go. Learn to surrender peacefully, or you will become a candidate for panic attacks.

6. A perfectionist who lives in an imperfect world, or a controlling person who lives in an out-of-control world. You are reading a book written by a perfectionist! When I was in college, I would take the change out of my pockets and carefully stack it according to denomination.

I like things to be neat, and I have a way to do everything. If you looked in my closet, you would see that everything has a place and that everything is in its place because I am a perfectionist. I know that people like me are candidates for panic attacks because we live in a very imperfect world. It was a good day for me when I let my car get dusty. It was a good day for me when I didn't worry about whether or not the suit was hung up just right. It was a good day for me when I didn't care whether or not my change was neatly stacked according to denomination! It would be a good day for some people to realize they live in a very imperfect world with a totally out-of-control environment.

7. Wives who must work full-time to help make ends meet. When the wife, who is a weaker vessel, feels the pressure that she has no other options, she is a classic candidate for panic attacks.

I am not a preacher who believes that it is wrong for women to work outside the home. To me the decision belongs to the husband and his wife. It is quite possible that she needs the fellowship of some good Christian workers. I do believe she needs to be extremely careful about the workplace atmosphere. Also, I don't think a wife should work outside the home unless she wants to work.

In our household, I told my wife that she would never have to work. Never one time did I ever tell her that she had to work because we needed some extra money. That was my decision, and at times I did some odd jobs. I poured concrete, worked in some construction, and even roofed houses so she would not need to work outside the home.

I would not make that decision for another household; you do what you want to do. My point is that when a husband tells his wife to go to work in order for him to be able to do what he wants to do, this decision places undue pressure on his wife. Frankly, I believe a person who forces his wife to work is setting the stage for her to deal with incredible emotional stress.

On the other hand, I am not opposed to a wife helping her husband by taking a job for a few years to help her husband when he is attending college. I am opposed when the husband forces his wife to go to work, and she has no option. He creates a pressure that could lead to anxiety and panic attacks.

8. Husbands who do not have the positive and verbal support and trust of their wives. Truthfully, a man really does not want a whole lot from his wife. Certainly, he wants affection and romance. What he wants most of all is for the one woman who knows him best to say, "I believe in you." When the one person who knows him best says, "I, the one who knows you best, believes in you the most," that man can conquer the world—his world. When a man does not have this emotional help, he is subject to episodes of panic.

9. Christians who have a secret world that is not consistent with their Christianity. Young adults can easily have a private world of indulging in drinking without getting caught, going to the movie theater without anyone knowing, and getting by with fornication. Just some simple planning and careful time management can create a secret world.

Even a Christian can have his Internet pornography via his laptop hidden away in his private office. He can secretly visit chat rooms and even have a vicarious liaison with some woman he has never met. To be sure, even a Christian can get by with having an indecent secret world for a little while.

Everyone can have a secret world, including me. I do have a secret word, but my secret world consists of walking with God. When I am not with my wife, I am walking with Him. If I am not walking with God, I am praying. My world consists of trying to take the world of First Baptist Church to the world. I do enjoy hunting and fishing with my son and son-in-law. I have a world that I enjoy with my family, but that's not a secret world. I strive to so live my life that if my secret world was ever exposed, the world would say, "Big deal!"

My point is not to show how good or how bad I am. I am a sinner, I have made mistakes, and I battle my besetting sins and weaknesses—just like every person. My point is: if your secret world is not in harmony with what the Bible says, that world is setting you up for anxiety attacks, panic disorders, and emotional problems later in life. You will be totally exhausted from the pressure of living a duplicitous life. It requires so much energy to play the part of a hypocrite. The more two-faced you are, the more energy you must expend with trying to keep all of your tracks covered and your lies consistent. When you get caught or when you suspect you are in danger of being caught, you are probably about to unravel. You have probably reached your limit, and your emotions are fragmented, your nerves are on end, and you don't understand why you are so emotionally distraught. Judas tried to live a double life. He chose a rope to put an end to his life—what a sad ending to a promising young man.

10. **Intense self-analysis.** All of the above-mentioned causes of panic attacks can be summarized in this one. The common thread that describes people having panic attacks is ME! A person will be as mentally unhealthy as he is consumed with wondering how he is doing.

The Bible says, "...*No man, having put his hand to the plow, and looking back, is fit for the kingdom of God."* (Luke 9:62) I have heard many preachers teach that this verse is addressing a man who starts something and quits. I am sure that is a part of the meaning, but the verse does not say that. It doesn't say *"turns back"*; it says *"looks back."*

My attention was arrested by this discovery. In this day, not many people are left who have tilled a field with a plow pulled by horses or mules. Through the years I have enjoyed hearing my dad tell stories about the times he plowed with workhorses. I asked him to explain this verse in light of his knowledge about farming with horses. He said, "You take a strong grip on that two-handled plow and hang on for dear life because a 1,500-pound workhorse is effortlessly pulling that plow. Your job is to keep that horse motivated and moving parallel to the other furrows. The only reason a man looks back is to see how he is doing."

How does that illustration pertain to the Christian? A Christian should not be constantly checking to see how he is doing. The person who constantly asks himself, "How do I measure up?" is opening the door to danger. He should not think he is a bad Christian, nor should he think he is a good Christian. He shouldn't even worry about what kind of Christian he is. Rather, he should be an obedient Christian, consumed with trying to get other people to become Christians! Stop worrying about how you are doing! Measuring yourself can bring on panic attacks and anxiety attacks because you are consumed with self-analysis.

"Am I as good as so-and-so?" How can I possibly know? I am not so-and-so, and God doesn't measure me by that person. *"For we dare not make ourselves of the number, or compare ourselves with some that commend themselves: but they measuring themselves by themselves, and comparing themselves among themselves, are not wise."* (II Corinthians 10:12) I am measured by my obedience to His Book and by my loyalty to my Saviour.

To be sure, every Christian should have a good sense of self-esteem, which means liking oneself, accepting oneself, and appreciating one's self-worth.

Self-esteem is built on accomplishment; that is, we feel good about ourselves when we can perform, accomplish, and act in ways that we value and desire to be. Anxiety tends to rob people of initiative and ability to take fulfilling action. A high degree of self-esteem is a major characteristic of successful coping with the anxieties and the stresses of everyday life. Almost anything that disrupts, colors, inhibits, or interferes with one's performance will affect self-esteem. This makes it all the more important to deal with anxieties.[6]

Eleanor Roosevelt said, "No one can make you feel inferior without your consent." It is your personal responsibility to react properly to what happens to you. Your ability to react properly determines whether or not you feel marvelous or miserable. Therein lies the ability to living with a healthy self-worth.

Practical Advice for Fighting Panic Attacks

1. **Exercise.** Some type of physical venting of a person's emotion is needed. Learn to vent properly through some cardiovascular workouts. Get your heart rate up. Don't get into stiff competition; rather, work at shaping and building your body. At the same time, do not become too preoccupied with how you look, which in itself can be emotionally unhealthy. Walking is a great, enjoyable form of exercise, as is tennis, bicycling, and gardening.

Exercise is also a very important activity while working on anxiety disorders because exercise not only helps process excess adrenaline but also helps you feel better, be less sensitized to body sensations that could trigger anxiety, and aids in self-confidence and willingness to face difficult issues and situations.[7]

2. Daily meditation. Take time everyday to think about the Word of God. Think about portions of Scripture, and think about how you can obey God's Word. Don't think about how you are doing as a Christian.

Meditation is effective in both reducing general stress and in helping to relax a body and a mind made tense by anxiety or worry. When you meditate, you quiet your nervous system, thereby reducing your heart rate and state of muscle contraction. When you meditate on a regular basis, you come away with more positive feelings after a stressful encounter, sleep better, and tackle your challenges with more confidence.[8]

3. Be a reader. Reading helps us to escape the pressures of life by entering into the vicarious world of good authors. I love going back in the 1800s and visiting some time zone I can no longer visit. I like sailing on the *Mayflower* and crossing the uncharted Atlantic Ocean with Christopher Columbus. I enjoy going on a hunting expedition or on an African safari. I like blazing the Oregon Trail with pioneer missionaries like Marcus and Narcissa Whitman, who were the first white people to cross the Rockies in a wagon. I like wrestling alligators in Florida. I like shooting snakes in Arizona. I like going partridge hunting in South Dakota.

I enjoy reading some fiction—dog stories and horse stories are captivating. I just enjoy reading! I get into books to take my mind away from the pressures I have to face every day. Reading allows me to take a collective deep breath. My mind can relax, and my emotions can enjoy a little recess.

4. Hobbies. My wife and I enjoy watching birds. We have 12 or 13 bird feeders at our house, and we watch for the hummingbirds to make their arrival in the spring. Some afternoons we sit at the table and take turns urging each other to look at a particular bird. If we notice a new one, we study our bird book and try to identify it. We are definitely into birding, but we also enjoy a variety of hobbies.

Take up a good hobby with your best friend, your spouse, or your family members. Kiting is great! We bought some fancy kites to fly in some of those deluxe, strong winds. We have gone kiting in some of the stiffest winds and had the time of our lives. Try bicycling. Take your family away from the television for a little while and do something enjoyable. You will feel good about yourself while indulging in a good hobby. Men, take your son to a pistol range and enjoy shooting together. Teach him the mechanics of how to handle a gun. A hobby is a good diversion.

> **A Quick Reference to Combat Anxiety:**
> 1—Slow down.
> 2—Have a short relaxation before eating—regular meals, good food.
> 3—Rest in the middle of the day.
> 4—Use breathing exercises.
> 5—Have plenty of fresh air, and get outdoor exercise.
> 6—Use positive self-talk.
> 7—Go to bed early.[9]

Life is not simply to be enjoyed, but don't forget to enjoy it while you are living it! Living is much too wonderful to be wasted by worrying about whether or not you are going to have a panic attack. What a waste of life!

CHAPTER SIX

God's Reaction to Rejection

Prerequisite Reading
Luke 14:16-24

Just because you believe the Bible does not mean that you are automatically immune from the pressures of living in this fast-paced society. If you neglect your body, if you fail to get the proper amount of rest, if you do not take care of your diet, and if you do not have a systematic walk with God, you will not maintain a good rhythm and cadence in life. As a result, you will be as susceptible to the same problems of anxiousness and fretting as are the unsaved.

> A healthy diet consists of 35 percent fruits and vegetables, 40 percent complex carbohydrates, 20 percent protein-rich food, and 5 percent fat.[1]

Every Christian has tremendous advantages over an unsaved person. He has the Spirit of the living God. He has access to Christian counselors, and he has the Word of God as his guide. Nonetheless, these anxious moments and panic disorders often attack even the best of Christians. Isaiah 26:3 says, *"Thou wilt keep him in perfect peace, whose mind is stayed on thee: because he trusteth in thee."* One way to keep cadence and peace in your life is to keep your mind focused on the Word of God.

"Great peace have they which love thy law: and nothing shall offend them." (Psalm 119:165) Perfect peace comes with freely offering forgiveness—no holds barred—forgiving everything.

Philippians 4:7 says, *"And the peace of God, which passeth all understanding, shall keep your hearts and minds through Christ Jesus."* Having the peace of God helps protect your heart and your mind. Many passages throughout the Bible address the subject of guarding or protecting your heart and mind.

The passage that is the focal point of this chapter does not seem to fit into the realm of peace verses like Isaiah 26:3, Psalm 119:165, and Philippians 4:7. However, if you will give me a good reading, I believe you will see that Luke 14 indeed fits with the subject of having peace.

Luke 14 contains the parable called "The Great Supper." In this story, we find emotions and feelings that come from God. So often, people try to "box" God into a certain scenario. They make statements like, "Well, this is the way God is!" or "This is what God says!" or "I know how God feels about this." As a matter of fact, God does choose at times to indicate how He feels about certain matters. In this particular parable, I believe God seems to be going through what might be described by psychologists as a classic case of rejection syndrome.

> Rejection is [defined as] being socially excluded or criticized which would produce considerable emotional pain and self-degradation. The avoidance of social situations may take obvious forms such as extreme shyness, avoidance of meeting new people, or avoiding parties and crowds. Individuals with extreme rejection generally have a low self-esteem.[2]

In this particular passage God is pictured as a man who has invited a great host of people he presumed to be his friends to a huge banquet or reception. Luke 14:16 says, *"Then said he unto him, A certain man made a great supper, and bade* [or invited] *many."* This particular Scripture provides us with a keen insight into the nature of God.

The Preparation

This man prepared a great supper, possibly a wedding reception. In May 2005 national news carried a story for several weeks about a bride who was supposedly kidnaped and left her groom "standing at the wedding altar." He was left to explain to approximately 600 guests why the wedding and reception were being cancelled. As I listened to the news reports, I tried to place myself in the shoes of those stricken people who believed that the bride had been kidnaped and taken against her will. Those who listened to any of the reports eventually heard the call that revealed the sham of the bride's story. Supposedly, she got "cold feet," and instead of just asking for a postponement, she made up a story of kidnaping that eventually involved the police and the FBI.

I tried to empathize with the parents when they learned that their daughter had been so deceitful. How do you call 600 guests and say, "There will be no wedding this week"? I tried to think how her fiancé felt. I tried to think about how the would-be bride would face the coming days of trying to reconcile her act of desperation. No doubt this would have been an emotional venture for all involved—one capable of producing great anxiety.

Just like this wedding story, the man in Luke 14 had also thoroughly prepared *"a great supper,"* and he had invited many, but not one person came. The word *great* in this context is the word "mega." It would be like preparing a Pastors' School or a Youth Conference and having no one come! This man must have felt tremendously abandoned.

My wife went to a wedding shower for a dear family, which was not scheduled at the best of times. Many other activities had also been scheduled for the same time. My wife came home and said, "I feel so terrible."

When I asked her what had happened, she said, "It was obvious that a lot of preparation went into the decorations and food. Only a small handful of people came. Just a handful of gifts were on the table designated for the gifts."

After she shared about the evening, I had such a deep sadness in my heart because I want every young lady to have a large wedding shower and a well-attended wedding. My wife's words caused me to think about one of my first weddings as pastor of First Baptist Church. I was walking with the groom and the best man, and we could smell the aromas of the food that was being prepared for the reception. I jokingly said, "That food smells so good; let's skip the wedding and go to the reception!"

"Brother Schaap," the groom excitedly said, "we've got tons of food because we are expecting a large crowd. I just hope we planned for enough."

When he made that statement, I could not help but cringe inwardly because the people of First Baptist Church are very busy people. So many activities take place on Saturdays: bus route visitation, big day preparations, soul-winning ministry meeting, and Sunday school visitation, just to name a few. We continued walking toward the Jack Hyles Memorial Auditorium, and we stopped to look through the one of the windows. Only a small handful of people had gathered for the wedding. His jaw just dropped.

I turned to him and said, "May I remind you why you are here today?"

Tears glistened in his eyes as he looked at me. I continued, "You are here for a precious lady who is going to be your wife. As long as she shows up, that's all that matters."

He said, "I guess so, but what am I going to do with all of that food?"

We tried to make what could have been a "sad" event into a happy one, but I will always remember the look on his face when he saw just a handful of people present for their wedding day.

I know something far worse! This man in Luke 14 prepared what I liken to a wedding reception, and absolutely no one came—not even the guest of honor! If indeed he had planned a wedding reception, not even the prospective bride and bridegroom attended! Not one guest came! Not only was he left with a lot of food, he also had to pay the bill. His preparation seemingly was in vain.

The Invitation

His invitation was sent to those he presumed he knew—family members, relatives, loved ones, friends, and co-workers. His invitation wasn't sent to just anyone; it went out to those he knew would come. This man had spent a lot of money. He had invited many people he knew should be there, and he knew the banquet hall would be full. For whatever reason, nobody came. No doubt this man felt a tremendous emotional rejection.

The Rejection

"The dictionary gives the very word "reject" some downbeat definitions, including: the refusal to accept or admit someone, the refusal to grant a request or a demand, and the discard of something useless or unsatisfactory (as in "We don't need you.") The noun "reject" (as in "You're just a reject on the scrap heap of life.") is a person or thing tossed away as unnecessary, unwanted, or imperfect."[3]

Luke 14:18 says, *"And they all with one consent began to make excuse. The first said unto him, I have bought a piece of ground...."* The second person the servant contacted said he had bought five yoke of oxen. The third said he had married a wife, and the excuses kept coming. In my mind, when you want something done bigtime, excuses never hold any water!

For me, holding the public services of First Baptist Church is a life-and-death issue. The people who attend church deserve a first-class sound system so they can hear the services. They deserve a clean building which looks first class. Everything in the church house should be exactly right because God's business is the greatest business in the world! Putting on a nationwide Pastors' School is not as important to me as the public services of First Baptist Church of Hammond, Indiana.

This man in Luke 14 had made costly preparations and had sent out exclusive invitations. Imagine his hurt when the excuses began to arrive.

A teacher of an adult Sunday school class was discussing his class with me. He mentioned that he had spent more money than usual on preparations for a big day. His statement caught my attention. "All big days are expensive," I interjected. "May I remind you that nothing you spent was more valuable than what Jesus paid for us to have a Sunday school class!"

Seeing people saved and baptized, having their lives changed, marriages healed, families reunited, and addicts delivered from their bondage is wonderful! God has trusted us with His business—the biggest business in all the world! In my mind, excuses don't hold up when lives are at stake. No excuse is a good excuse.

In this portion of Scripture, Jesus Christ is saying that His Father prepared a huge feast called salvation. He sent His invitation for salvation to all of the religious leaders of that day—the Pharisees, the Sadducees, and the scribes. The Father just knew that those who spent their days and nights studying the Word of God would love to come to salvation. He knew that the theologians and legal lawyers would love to come and take of salvation. Surely those who spent their lifetime memorizing the books of the Bible would love to come. Sadly, every one of them gave an excuse as to why he could not come. The best analogy I can make is a father giving his daughter her dream wedding, and no one attending—not even the daughter!

Just a year and four months after I became pastor of First Baptist Church, I gave my daughter away in marriage. As we stepped into the Jack Hyles Memorial Auditorium to make our walk to the altar, we saw the place was filled. Of course, I knew then that some kindly came because "It's the pastor's daughter, and we need to be there. After all, he performs weddings for our children. We need to show our support."

I think that some meetings are obligatory, and probably that is good. Sometimes people should attend certain events because it's right to do. God felt sure that certain people would be obliged to come to His reception. After all, He was God, and He had offered His Son as the Saviour of the world. He couldn't believe it when no one came! How disappointed and rejected He must have felt. "Some common post-rejection reactions are numbness, shock, and denial; anger, rage, and the desire for revenge; embarrassment, humiliation, and shame; depression and self-blame; and a need for action to relive the feelings."[4]

We can understand the mind of God in this matter. How disappointed we are when the people we lean on and count on don't come through for us. How disappointed we are when we go soul winning, and for whatever reason, a person discounts his need for salvation.

The Passion

Luke 14:21 says, "*So that servant came, and shewed his lord these things* [the excuses]. *Then the master of the house being angry said to his servant, Go out quickly...*" Notice what rejection caused in this man who represents God the Father. Rejection is an emotional wound that elicits a powerful reaction. In other words, God hurts deeply when men reject His invitation.

When a person is invited to get saved, and he indifferently says, "I don't want to," God said, "That hurts Me!" God hurts deeply when He orchestrates events to send a soul winner to get someone saved, and that person refuses His invitation. His is not a passive emotion; He feels great hurt and rejection.

Rejection is an emotion that God understands very well. Perhaps a parent or a close family member abused you, and as a result, you felt terribly rejected. Deep emotional hurts reside deep in the inner recesses of your being that you have tried to forget.

Each experience of neglect, or physical, sexual, or emotional abuse a child feels causes further damage to a child's sense of self. When children have experienced this degree of rejection, they may begin to reject themselves.[5]

You have a God in Heaven Who understands the emotions of rejection! *"For we have not an high priest which cannot be touched with the feeling of our infirmities; but was in all points tempted like as we are, yet without sin."* (Hebrews 4:15)

I received a letter from a young lady who was agonizing over her father's continual rejection. She wrote, "The more I reach out to him, the more he pushes me away. I would love for Daddy just one time to put his arms around me and say, 'I sure am glad you're my daughter.'" And she said, "I don't know where to go to get that." I personally do not believe that father could do a more damaging work in his daughter's life than to push her away!

Abandonment by a parent is one of the most powerful kinds of rejection that can happen to a child. Rejection can vary in degree from mild to severe. Abandonment by or loss of a parent is on the highest-impact end.[6]

I couldn't help but think of my family. All of our immediate family members and my parents were together for a Sunday meal. Our granddaughter Lyndsay was being passed around. She went from my daughter to my son-in-law, back to his wife (my daughter), and then to my wife. As my wife was holding Lyndsay, my mother said, "What a fortunate child to be touched and loved by so many people who dearly love her."

For those who come from families where you were touched and loved, how fortunate you are! Rejoice if you are a member of a church where you receive a lot of love from a lot of people. First Baptist Church of Hammond is not a one-dimensional ministry. People who come to First Baptist Church are loved by many, and they do not need to feel rejected because of deep inner hurts. People do not have to understand your hurts because He understands! He totally understands that feeling of rejection; after all, He prepared a fabulous reception and invited many guests. Every place setting had a name plate by it. Every empty seat became a reminder that someone felt he had something more important to do than come to His reception.

Our great God wonders what is more important than showing up at the foot of the cross. God does not want to hear all the sorry excuses that people offer. See the heart of a God Who says, "I know you have been rejected." He knows about that past hurt and wounding from molestation and the emotional damage that has invaded your heart. He understands the intense rejection because He was rejected too. God became angered by that rejection. The passion of rejection is anger.

The Persuasion

Luke 14:21 says, *"So that servant came, and showed his lord these things. Then the master of the house being angry said to his servant, Go out quickly into the streets and lanes of the city, and bring in hither the poor, and the maimed, and the halt, and the blind."* It is thrilling to me to know that God wanted the people who felt rejected to come to the banquet! He sent servants to find those who did not fit in because they were poor and could not afford nice gifts and those who were high-maintenance—the blind, the maimed, and the afflicted, if you please. He sent invitations to those who required an incredible amount of attention.

The best medicine for the one who feels rejected is to find and love the crowd that nobody else wants. That is exactly how God had to deal with His rejection! He sent His Son to earth for 33 years. For three and one-half years, He walked among the theologians who supposedly knew the Bible. As a matter of fact, the scribes and Pharisees had even memorized the first five books of the Bible by the time they were seven years old! They should have been excitedly looking for the Great Prophet, but they rejected Him when He came. With His rejection came the invitation to those who could not read, study, and memorize the Word of God. He sent His servants to find the rejected ones. Still, the rejected ones had to be compelled to come to the reception because they knew nobody wanted them.

The reason we work so hard at First Baptist Church to bring in the people of Chicagoland is because we want them to know a God Who knows what it feels like to be rejected, and we want them to have one place where they feel very accepted. We want them to have a place of comfort and acceptance. I want First Baptist Church to be like a tidal wave of love washing over people. When a person's home is a place of rejection, where emotions of anger and bitterness are always present and where he does not feel loved or accepted, he must have a place of acceptance. That place of acceptance must be in the church house!

The persuasion is to get those who feel rejected. Reach the children who feel rejected by their mom and dad! Reach the teenagers who feel rejected by their peers because they look a little different or their clothes have a different label. How sad to reject another human being because of the wrong labels, the wrong neighborhood, or the wrong crowd. God understands how the rejected ones feel. *"He is despised and rejected of men…and we hid as it were our faces from him…."* (Isaiah 53:3) People who have been neglected, and rejected, and abused, and violated, and hurt, and wounded have a Saviour Who says, *"Come unto me, all ye that labour and are heavy laden, and I will give you rest."* (Matthew 11:28)

According to Ephesians 1:4-6, one of the wonderful gifts that you receive when you trust Christ as your Saviour is acceptance in the beloved. God will make us feel as accepted as if we were Jesus Christ, the Son of God Himself. God loves us as much as He loves His only Child.

The Purpose

"And the servant said, Lord, it is done as thou hast commanded, and yet there is room. And the lord said unto the servant, Go out into the highways and hedges, and compel them to come in, that my house may be filled." (Luke 14:22, 23) The purpose of our going out is to try to fill God's house because every empty seat is a reminder to God that someone has something better to do.

I would never have chosen to build the new 7,500-seat auditorium. I loved preaching behind the pulpit of Dr. Jack Hyles every week. I was very comfortable in the church built by my father-in-law. However, when we voted to build the new auditorium, I said in my heart, "God, a larger auditorium will be our opportunity to show You more people love You."

When the Jack Hyles Memorial Auditorium was built, it was not jam-packed full for many years. When it was finally filled to overflowing, we had to turn people away from the services. Brother Hyles had added seats in every conceivable place possible, and he had added closed-circuit televisions for the overflow crowd. Every time I walked in to see the building filled to overflowing, I would say, "God, do You feel loved? Your house is full." I felt that a full church house was a way for our people to say to God, "We haven't made any excuses; we're here!"

I want the same to happen eventually in our building at 473 Sibley. Within the next few years, I want this building to get fuller and fuller and fuller. Someday, I want us to see people jam-packed into both of the overflow rooms, chairs in the aisles, and chairs in the hallways to hold the crowds. That is our purpose!

Why? Because I personally want to have 10,000 in church? Of course not! I want God, Who feels the rejection of a world that is too busy for Him and too involved in all their sports, games, toys, and entertainment, to say, "There's a place in Hammond filled with people who have been rejected, abandoned, and hurt. I feel welcome in that church!" First Baptist Church always must strive to be a place where everyone feels accepted and welcomed—even God.

Certainly God likes a full church house; our great Redeemer does not like to see the evidence of rejection.

- When the movie theater is full, and the church house is half full, how is God supposed to feel?
- When the stadium is filled for a rock concert or a sporting event, but the church house is half empty, how is God supposed to feel?
- When the living rooms are filled on Sunday nights or Wednesday nights with people who are too busy or too tired to go to church, but not so busy or tired that they can't watch the television, how is God supposed to feel?
- When the stadium is filled with people who want to see a ball game or go to a Nascar race, but the church house is empty, how is God supposed to feel?

He commanded His servants, "Go out and find guests so that My house may be filled!" God wants a full house, and I want to do my part in giving Him what He wants! Let's not be a part of rejecting God.

As you deal with your own personal rejection and feelings of anger and bitterness within you, please consider the following:

1. Don't seek to punish those who have rejected you. Jesus didn't say, "Round up all the people who rejected Me and kill them." No! He said, "Let's go get someone else." Too many people stay too busy trying to exert justice when it is not in their hands to exert justice.

In the essay "The Classroom Avenger," Baltimore police psychologist James McGee writes about lifestyles and personality traits characteristic of the seventeen teenagers who killed forty-five students and teachers (and wounded eighty-five others) in school murders, beginning in 1993 and ending after fifteen people were killed at Columbine High School in Littleton, Colorado, in 1999. According to the study, all of the killers considered themselves social outcasts who had suffered from teasing and victimization by educators and other students. They were all overly sensitive to criticism or rejection and had found the most negative way imaginable to deal with their feelings.[7]

Let me be perfectly honest with you. If you do succeed in hurting the one who hurt you, it will not make your hurt go away. You will still have the wounds and the scars. If you violate the one who hurt you in the same way you were violated, all it would do is make you feel as cheap as they feel. We must let go of the anger and forgive.

According to *Merriam Webster's Collegiate Dictionary*, to *forgive* is to "pardon an offense or an offender" or to "cease to feel resentment against." But forgiveness is more than the dictionary definition. Forgiveness is the key to healing and a way to avoid becoming filled with bitterness. Forgiveness is a way to get over rejection and to quit being a victim. Forgiveness is letting go of the past. Forgiveness is a gift to someone you believe has done you wrong. Forgiveness is a gift to yourself. Forgiveness is a way of getting rid of the anger that otherwise stays bottled up inside of you. Forgiveness is nonjudgmental. Forgiveness is a deep breath followed by a feeling of relief.

Forgiveness does not mean you have to announce it to the world or to those you have forgiven. Even without your announcement, they will probably notice the difference in your attitude. Forgiveness does not mean letting the person get away without confrontation or consequences. A person who commits a crime against you may have to serve jail time. But you can forgive that person. Forgiveness is not denying your pain or any of your other feelings, including anger. However, people who have complained of chronic headaches, stomachaches, and other aches after a rejection often notice that the pain disappears when they forgive. Forgiveness does not automatically require you to heal a relationship.[8]

2. Seek to accept those who have been rejected. A lost world does not need your bitterness; rather, your acceptance of God's love is what is desperately needed. Walking around with a chip on your shoulder and a Gospel tract in your hand does not coincide. A world that has no answers does not need your foul spirit; a lost world needs the grace of our Lord Jesus Christ. *"For by grace are ye saved...."* When you exhibit God's grace, you are the carrier of His grace.

That grace is why people loved to hear Brother Hyles preach and loved be around him. He graciously infused those who surrounded him with an infectious kindness. A person who buoys the spirits of others makes them feel like better people.

The man who prepared the reception became angry, but he realized his anger was to no avail. He decided instead to fill the reception hall with the rejects, the halt, the maimed, the blind, and the deaf—those who needed to feel accepted. He realized that was the only way that he would feel accepted!

3. Bring the rejected ones to Jesus. If you want healing for your rejected teenage years, if you want to make up for the heartache that somebody inflicted on you when you were an adolescent, if you want to make up for the fact that you were introduced to liquor or abuse when you were a teenager, find someone else who has been rejected and bring that person to a place of acceptance. Bring the person to the Saviour Who knows what it is like to be rejected. Jesus can make all the difference.

I believe if you would work as much at bringing the rejected people of this world to Jesus Christ as you do with visiting multiple doctors, psychologists, counselors, clinics, symposiums, and other professionals, you could put the past and its inner hurts behind you. None of these professionals, with all their studies and therapies, can fix the past. For this study, I have read copious amounts of materials from many sources. Every one of these sources offers basically the same help but is worded somewhat differently. These professionals tell the person to make positive changes, look your best, live with your decisions, be healthy, be happy, laugh a lot because laughter has physical and emotional benefits, work out and exercise, eat well, get enough rest, get busy, relax, meditate, be mindful, avoid unhealthy distractions, break unhealthy relationships, get support, and confide. Rejection does not have to be the end of the world! The truth is that no human being can heal all of the inner hurts, but we have a Saviour Who can! H. H. Joy said it beautifully in his song, "All Your Anxiety."

"Is there a heart o'erbound by sorrow?
Is there a life weighed down by care?
Come to the cross, each burden bearing,
All your anxiety—leave it there.

No other Friend so keen to help you;
No other Friend so quick to hear,
No other place to leave your burden;
No other one to hear your prayer.

Come then, at once, delay no longer;
Heed His entreaty, kind and sweet;

You need not fear a disappointment,
You shall find peace at the Mercy Seat.

All your anxiety, all your care,
Bring to the Mercy Seat, leave it there;
Never a burden He cannot bear,
Never a friend like Jesus."

Endnotes

Foreword

[1] http://www.Association of American Physicians and Surgeons.online.org.

[2] http://www.pbs.org/wgbh/nova/doctors.

[3] Tracy Alderman, Ph.D., *The Scarred Soul: Understanding and Ending Self-Inflicted Violence* (Oakland, Calif.: New Harbinger Publications, Inc., 1997), 97.

[4] *Ibid.*, 107-108.

Chapter One

[1] Jan Sutton and Deb Martenson, *Because I Hurt* (n.c.: How-To Books, 2006).

[2] http://www.samaritanministries.com.

[3] http://www.coolnurse.com/self-injury.html.

[4] Alicia Clarke, M.A., *Coping with Self-Mutilation: A Helping Book for Teens Who Hurt Themselves* (New York: The Rose Publishing Group, Inc., 1999), 2.

[5] Mary A. Fischer, "Thrills that Kill," *Reader's Digest*, February, 2006, 120-21.

[6] Alderman, 221.

[7] http://www.National Mental Health Organization, help guide.org.

[8] Clarke, 11.

[9] Alderman, 24.

[10] Cherry Boone O' Neill, *Starving for Attention* (New York: Continuum Publishing Company, 1982), 168.

[11] Alderman, 92.

[12] *Ibid.*, 19.

[13] Michel Hersen and Alan S. Bellack, *Psychopathology in Adulthood* (Needham Heights, Mass.: A Pearson Education Company, 2000), 410.

[14] Gabriel Cousens, M.D., with Mark Mayell, *Depression-Free for Life: An All-Natural, 5-Step Plan to Reclaim Your Zest for Living* (New York: Harper Collins Publishers, Inc., 2000), 46.

[15] Clarke, 41.

[16] Alderman, 95.

[17] *Ibid.*, 46.

[18] Dena Rosenbloom, Ph.D. and Mary Beth Williams, Ph.D., with Barbara E. Watkins, *Life After Trauma: A Workbook for Healing* (New York: The Guilford Press, 1999), 194.

[19] Harold H. Bloomfield, M.D., and Peter McWilliams, *How to Heal Depression* (Los Angeles: Prelude Press, 1994), 152.

[20] *Ibid.*, 142.

Chapter Three

[1] Jenny Petrak and Barbara Hedge, Editors, *The Trauma of Sexual Assault: Treatment, Prevention, and Practice* (New York: John Wiley and Sons, Inc., 2002, 112.

[2] *Ibid.*

Chapter Four

[1] Shirley Trickett, *Anxiety and Depression: A Natural Approach* (Berkeley, Calif.: Ulysses Press, 2001), 7.

[2] American Psychiatric Association, *Diagnostic and Statistical Manual of Mental Disorders, Fourth Edition, Text Revision* (Washington, DC: American Psychiatric Association, 2000), 432.

[3] Jennifer Shoquist, M.D. and Diane Stafford, *No More Panic Attacks* (Franklin Lakes, N.J.: Career Press, Inc., 2002), 12-13.

[4] *Ibid.*, 21.

[5] *Ibid.*, 32.

[6] Denise Beckfield, Ph.D, *Master Your Panic and Take Back Your Life!* (San Luis Obispo, Calif.: Impact Publishers, 1994), 33.

[7] Sarah Lennard-Brown, *Stress and Depression* (Austin, Tex.: Steck-Vaughn Company, 2001), 15.

[8] Mitch Albom, "I Cannot Read," *Chicago Tribune Parade*, Sunday, 12 February, 2006, 7.

[9] Lennard-Brown, 20-21.

[10] Shoquist and Stafford, 22.

[11] Beckfield, 16-17.

[12] Ada P. Kahn, Ph.D., and Ronald M. Doctor, Ph.D., *Facing Fears: The Sourcebook for Phobias, Fears, and Anxieties* (New York: Checkmark Books, 2000) 53.

[13] Petrak and Hedge, 162-163.

[14] James Lawrence Thomas, Ph.D., with Christine A. Adamec, *Do You Have Attention Deficit Disorder?* (New York: Dell Publishing, 1996), 215-225

Chapter Five

[1] Beckfield, 80-81.

[2] American Psychiatric Association, 466.

[3] Kahn and Doctor, 220-21.

[4] Jane S. Ferber, M.D., with Suzanne LeVert, *A Woman Doctor's Guide to Depression* (New York: Hyperion Press, 1997), 26.

[5] Rosenbloom and Williams, 43.

[6] Kahn and Doctor, 74-75.

[7] *Ibid.*, 85.

[8] Ferber, 160-61.

[9] Trickett, 124.

Chapter Six

[1] Lennard-Brown, 25.

[2] Kahn and Doctor, 231.

[3] Barbara Moe, *Coping With Rejection* (New York: The Rosen Publishing Group, Inc., 2001), 1-2.

[4] *Ibid.*, 17.

[5] *Ibid.*, 7.

[6] *Ibid.*, 6-7.

[7] *Ibid.*, 18.

[8] *Ibid.*, 45-46.

Sources Consulted

Albom, Mitch. "I Cannot Read." *Chicago Tribune Parade.* Sunday, 12 February, 2006.

Alderman, Tracy, Ph.D. *The Scarred Soul: Understanding and Ending Self-Inflicted Violence.* Oakland, Calif.: New Harbinger Publications, Inc., 1997.

American Psychiatric Association. *Diagnostic and Statistical Manual of Mental Disorders, Fourth Edition, Text Revision.* Washington, DC: American Psychiatric Association, 2000.

Association of American Physicians and Surgeons.online.org.

Beckfield, Denise, Ph.D. *Master Your Panic and Take Back Your Life!* San Luis Obispo, Calif.: Impact Publishers, 1994.

Bloomfield, Harold H., M.D., and Peter McWilliams. *How to Heal Depression.* Los Angeles: Prelude Press, 1994.

Clarke, Alicia, M.A. *Coping with Self-Mutilation: A Helping Book for Teens Who Hurt Themselves.* New York: The Rose Publishing Group, Inc., 1999.

http://www.coolnurse.com/self-injury.html.

Cousens, Gabriel, M.D., with Mark Mayell. *Depression-Free for Life: An All-Natural, 5-Step Plan to Reclaim Your Zest for Living.* New York: HarperCollins Publishers, Inc., 2000.

Craig, Kenneth D. and Keith S. Dobson, Editors. *Anxiety and*

Depression in Adults and Children. Thousand Oaks, Calif.: Sage Publications, Inc., 1995.

Ferber, Jane S., M.D., with Suzanne LeVert. *A Woman Doctor's Guide to Depression*. New York: Hyperion Press, 1997.

Fischer, Mary A. "Thrills that Kill." *Reader's Digest*. February, 2006.

Hersen, Michel and Alan S. Bellack. *Psychopathology in Adulthood*. Needham Heights, Mass.: A Pearson Education Company, 2000.

Lee, Jordan. *Coping with Anxiety and Panic Attacks*. New York: The Rosen Publishing Group, Inc., 2000.

Lennard-Brown, Sarah. *Stress and Depression*. Austin, Tex.: Steck-Vaughn Company, 2001.

Kahn, Ada P., Ph.D. and Ronald M. Doctor, Ph.D. *Facing Fears: The Sourcebook for Phobias, Fears, and Anxieties*. New York: Checkmark Books, 2000.

Moe, Barbara. *Coping with Rejection*. New York: The Rosen Publishing Group, Inc., 2001.

National Mental Health Organization. helpguide.org.

http://www.pbs.org/wgbh/nova/doctors.

Petrak, Jenny and Barbara Hedge. *The Trauma of Sexual Assault: Treatment, Prevention, and Practice*. New York: John Wiley & Sons, Inc., 2002.

O'Neill, Cherry Boone. *Starving for Attention*. New York: Continuum Publishing Company, 1982.

Rosenbloom, Dena, Ph.D. and Mary Beth Williams, Ph.D. with Barbara Watkins. *Life After Trauma: A Workbook for Healing*. New York: The Guilford Press, 1999.

http://www.Samaritanministries.com.

Shoquist, Jennifer, M.D. and Diane Stafford. *No More Panic Attacks*. Franklin Lakes, N.J.: Career Press, Inc., 2002.

Sutton, Jan and Deb Martenson. *Because I Hurt*. n.c.: How-To Books, 2006.

Thomas, James Lawrence, Ph.D. with Christine A. Adamec. *Do You Have Attention Deficit Disorder?* (New York: Dell Publishing, 1996.

Trickett, Shirley. *Anxiety and Depression: A Natural Approach*. Berkeley, Calif.: Ulysses Press, 2001.

Wasmer Smith, Linda. *Depression: What It Is, How to Beat It*. Berkeley Heights, N.J.: Enslow Publishers, Inc., 2000.